# THE RUBBER ORCHESTRA

THE

# Rubber Orchestra

A MEMOIR IN TWO VOICES

## Nancy Johnson

*May 2001*

Life can be wonderful. And it can be horrific. What gets you through the most difficult times are love, help, and the willingness to fight.

This memoir by my late wife, Nancy Johnson, is about all of that — and more. It addresses the almost incomprehensible series of events that happened to us, our family, and our friends from August 2002 through June 2006.

I cannot overstate our gratitude to everyone who helped us then and since. Some are mentioned in this book; many are not. We are grateful to them all.

In January 2012, as Nancy was finishing this memoir, she died of ovarian cancer. (Her cancer had returned a few years earlier.) So the life together she spoke of at the end of this book did not last as long as we hoped. But, even after everything told here, we all had six more years together.

You will understand how lucky we were to have them.

On August 17, 2011, the twentieth anniversary of our wedding, Nancy wrote:

*The history we share is extraordinary, nothing we could have imagined. Who imagines that your future includes each of you facing death — truly facing death? It is too much to even think about. The blank slate has been colored in with trauma, grave trauma — and also great happiness. Life at the poles is our story, life served up with intense passion and emotion.*

None of us knows what happens to people after they die. I was taught that they are gone, but they live on in the good they do, as well as the love and joy they leave in others' hearts and minds. In addition to the good that Nancy did — and the love and joy she left — Nancy left us this book. That should add significantly to all three.

It should also make clear why she will be living on for a long, long time.

*— Arthur Bryant*

THE RUBBER ORCHESTRA

We are a rubber orchestra, gaining momentum in our final grab at summer. The soles of my running shoes slap the blacktop — macadam, high tops, hi-hat. The wheels of Arthur's and Wally's bicycles whir — woodwinds on the path. Wally, seven years old, starts school on Wednesday. Today we crescendo down a trail in Sunriver, a resort on the dry side of Oregon's Cascade Mountains. Even though my husband, Arthur, has been here working for several days, at this moment we are free.

Wally slows to ride even with me.

"Can we go swimming later, Mom?"

He wants the schedule to include all sports and no meals. Lean and tan, he likes to plan his days in advance, so he can have the excitement of looking forward. I watch the sweat bead on the bridge of his nose; he must be hot with all that curly hair stuffed under his helmet.

"We could go to the pool or hike or take out a paddle-boat, if you want," I say.

"Is a paddleboat like a canoe? That canoe yesterday was way too slow. I got bored. I mean, I liked the ducks and fish, and I liked playing on the shore of the lake, but I didn't want to just keep looking at the mountains forever. I'd rather go to the pool."

"Like father, like son," I say. "Although Daddy wouldn't have put a toe in a canoe."

"It's not my fault I get seasick in rocking boats," says

Arthur, who has slowed his bicycle to catch up on the conversation. He is sweating too, another case of curls-in-his-helmet, although if he is peddling hard enough to sweat, it might help him shed some of those I-like-food-too-much pounds.

"A canoe is hardly a rocking boat," I say.

"It's close enough for me. Why don't we grab some lunch? What do you think, Wallster?"

"Can we get sushi?" says Wally.

"Again?" I say.

We pedal and slap our way to the village at Sunriver, where, after lunch of, yes, sushi, I find a store with Halloween candles: orange-and-black-striped barber poles with black spiders climbing toward the wicks. I buy eight of them, thinking we will have a party this year. We had some great Halloween parties when we lived in Washington, D.C., but we haven't had one in the three years we've lived in Oakland. Arthur has been busy setting up the West Coast office of his public inter-est law firm and I've been getting Wally settled, teach-ing poetry at his school, training for a marathon, and working on a book.

Arthur is the executive director of the law firm, which means he carries out his management duties from the new office in California and travels back to the main office in D.C. an average of one week each month. The firm wanted more of a presence in the West and was already involved in a number of cases here. I too wanted to be back in the West, having moved to D.C. from Tucson. The eight years we spent in D.C. were enough for me. The nation's capital is an industry town, and I didn't want to be part of the industry. I also wanted Wally to grow up closer to the California Redwoods, the Sonoran Desert, Monument Valley, Zion, Bryce and Arches Parks and, truth be told, I wanted beauty. The San Francisco Bay Area, with its temperate climate and expansive views of water and mountains, is a beautiful place to live.

Before Arthur took this job, I didn't even know what a public interest law firm was. Turns out, it is just what it sounds like: a firm that takes cases in the public interest, where lots of people can be affected. They have represented kids suffering from lead paint poisoning, people who live in mobile homes with defective, leaky plumbing, and clients chewed up by propellers in boating accidents. They have sued car manufacturers for failing to install air bags, credit card companies that have cheated customers, and polluters nationwide.

Arthur has been here in Sunriver for the Oregon Trial Lawyers Association convention, trying to raise awareness and money for his firm. Wally and I caught the last days of summer in the mountains, but now it's time to go home. We plan to get up about seven o'clock tomorrow morning, so we can get the car packed to head back to Oakland. The drive should take eight hours. That will give us time to get Wally into bed by eight or eight thirty tomorrow night, so he will be ready for his first day in second grade.

The day is spectacular in that Oregon way: gas molecules in the atmosphere have done their job, absorbed the light and turned it into an almost painful clear blue. Sunlight shatters the branches of Douglas fir and Ponderosa pine, scattering shadows onto the ground. Inside our cabin, I take my time gathering fruit, water, and pretzels to bring along in the car for snacks. I pack up the laptops, odds and ends from the refrigerator, miscellaneous socks that Wally has left lying on various surfaces. I want to enjoy this space a little longer before we head into the rhythm of a long car ride. Arthur and Wally are loading my 1993 Toyota Corolla station wagon. This isn't too big a job. They just have to make sure nothing slides around in the back of the car and, after the hatch is closed, they have to attach the bike rack and bicycles.

We get started later than we intend but are still pretty much on schedule, so we can take our time getting home. Arthur starts out driving because he can't read in a moving car and I can. I settle in with *The Amazing Adventures of Kavalier & Clay*, but mostly I'm looking out my side window, enjoying the movement of light. There aren't many buildings along this road. I am content to watch the forest rustle as we pass. Wally sits behind me with his headphones on, listening to the singer most lately popular with the elementary school crowd. *Eric Clapton Unplugged* is on the car stereo.

By ten o'clock we are heading south on Highway 97, a two-lane string of road that stretches north-south through Oregon. Arthur is driving at the top of the 55-mph speed limit since there isn't much traffic and the road is clear. It feels like a day made for travel and soaking up the season's last bits of leisure. He and I talk about how much we like the people we know in Oregon and that it would be a great place to live except for the rain. We segue to how much we like living in the Bay Area. Just as we pass through the village of La Pine, thirty-four-year-old Christopher Adney, who is heading north, realizes he has missed the entrance to his driveway and whips his wheel left to make a fast turn across the road. This split-second movement slams his Chevy Silverado 4x4 pickup truck into our station wagon.

He blows us apart.

Time slows down for us as our car propels into the air, spinning around and over and filling with dust the impact has sucked up from the road and its shoulder. The sound of the impact reverberates as the car first lands on its roof, and then, deliberately and slowly, rights itself. The air swirls brown with dirt that fills all the open space. As the car falls back to earth, flames erupt from its engine.

The car's one air bag, on the driver's side, detonates, blowing out against Arthur's face and neck. The force of the crash has pushed the engine of the car backward into the interior. Its metal body folds around Arthur. The steering wheel pins his chest; the dashboard, with the engine behind it, crushes his legs.

My head and neck snap forward into the dashboard and then back against the seat, causing the seat itself to fly into Wally's legs. The front window comes crashing in. The rearview mirror slams into the left side of my forehead, and pieces of glass lodge themselves in my face and neck. The car's metal body breaks and slices into my left leg. The dashboard smashes into my right knee. I twist around to look at Wally; his stunned eyes are open wide and turn my head back. My screams cut the air.

Robert Carter, the first person to the scene, stops his car and runs over to our station wagon. He sees the engine on fire, and his impulse is to get people out if he can before the car explodes. Wally, alert in the backseat, responds to Mr. Carter's yelling to unlock his door and manages to pull up the lock. Carter pries open the door, unlatches the seat belt and grabs Wally under the arms to pull him out of the burning car. Wally falls as soon as he reaches ground. His leg is broken; Mr. Carter carries him to the side of the road.

Paramedics, firefighters, and police arrive quickly. Traffic has already begun backing up on both sides of the road, which will remain closed for hours. The firefighters extinguish the engine fire and then work to get Arthur and me out of the wreck. Wally is lying on a board, roadside, on top of thistles and dried grass and rocks.

Mr. Adney is also lying on the ground. He had not been wearing a seat belt, and the impact propelled him through the passenger's side front window of his truck and out onto the street. Although he says he doesn't need to go, he is driven in an ambulance to a nearby hospital.

State police at the scene charge him with three violations: driving without a license, driving without insurance, and driving without a seat belt.

Emergency workers disentangle me from the new metal-and-glass sculpture formerly known as my car and put me on a stretcher close to Wally. He can see me, but I am unconscious and bloody from my head wounds. We are waiting for the medivac helicopter. As soon as it arrives, we are loaded on and flown to St. Charles Medical Center in Bend, Oregon, the nearest trauma hospital.

Arthur's rescue, however, is not speedy. He is trapped in the driver's seat, the car enveloping his legs and torso. Emergency personnel work for over two hours. They remove the car door, cut away the metal they can, and finally use the Jaws of Life to pry Arthur from the car. His body is broken and smashed. No one imagines he will survive. He is also flown to St. Charles.

After Arthur is out of the car, emergency workers search for clues to our identities. Our possessions, including my purse and Arthur's wallet, which he habitually takes out of his pocket and lays on the console as he drives, are strewn along the highway. Someone rifles through the pockets of Arthur's pants, cut off when the emergency crew was trying to get him out of the car, and finds a folded-up piece of paper on which the name *Jeff Foote* and a phone number are written. This paper finds its way to a social worker at St. Charles, who calls the number.

When his cell phone rings, Jeff is in Mississippi, driving to the airport to catch a plane back to his home in

Portland, Oregon. The caller identifies himself as a social worker from the St. Charles Medical Center in Bend. He tells Jeff we were involved in an accident and asks him if he knows how to contact our family members. Jeff replies that Arthur's law offices, either in Oakland or Washington, D.C., would have numbers for Arthur's family and that he thinks Arthur's parents live in Pennsylvania.

The social worker also asks if there is anyone who lives close to Bend who might be able to come to stay with Wally, who was injured but is conscious. Jeff suggests Susan Saladoff, whose family was with ours at Sunriver and whose daughters babysat Wally while we were there. Susan lives in Ashland, Oregon.

Jeff says he's heading home to Portland and will drive down to the hospital early the next morning, and, even though he presses for it, the social worker won't give him any information about injuries to Arthur or me.

Susan Saladoff 's assistant is waiting by the door to grab her when she returns from lunch.

"Susan, I tried to reach you on your cell phone, but you didn't have it with you," the assistant says. "Mr. Bryant has been in a traffic accident and is badly hurt. They need you to call the hospital."

"Who?" says Susan, trying to place a Mr. Bryant.

"Mr. Bryant!" says her assistant. "Mr. Bryant!"

Then it hits her.

"Oh, my god," says Susan. "Arthur."

Susan phones the social worker, who asks her if she is able to come to the medical center right away. He tells her family members can't get to Oregon until tomorrow, Wednesday, and everyone is worried about Wally being alone because Arthur and Nancy are both unconscious. He tells her the accident was very serious and that, "we don't know what will happen."

Susan immediately calls her husband and tells him what's going on. They each arrange to leave work and then contact their two daughters. Their older daughter is in play rehearsals and can stay with a friend until they return from Bend. Their younger daughter, Dana, who is twelve, will go with them. Since she has recently spent time with Wally, the Saladoffs think it might be helpful to him to see a familiar, young face.

The drive from Ashland to Bend takes about three hours, and part of the route traces Highway 97. Even though they arrive at the crash site seven hours after the accident, crews are still clearing the area. When Susan sees our car, she doesn't believe either Arthur or I have survived. They pull off to the side of the road, and as Susan starts to get out, she clicks into autopilot. She's a lawyer, so she looks for information. She talks to fire personnel, police. One officer tells her that Mr. Adney said he realized he had missed his turn and at the last minute made a quick swerve to get into his driveway. The officer asked him if he didn't see Bryant's oncoming car, and Adney said no, he'd been looking in his rearview mirror.

Since she is the first friend or family member at the scene, the police allow Susan to take our personal effects. She and her family pick up everything they think we will want — computers, Arthur's briefcase, backpacks, clothing, underwear that has been strewn on the highway. Then Susan looks into the Toyota and sees Wolfie — Wally's friend who goes with him everywhere — a brown wolf puppet whose fur is ratty and missing in places. His black eyes are dull from washing, and now he is covered with dust and glass shards. Susan picks him up, shakes him off, and holds onto him as they drive to the medical center.

By the time they arrive at the hospital, it is a quarter after six. They are told that Arthur is in surgery and I am unconscious. Susan is concerned with getting to Wally, so he isn't so alone. He is in a private room, and as soon as they say hello and he recognizes them, he starts screaming: "Why did we have to go today? Where are my mom and dad? Why did that bad man do this to us?"

No one has answers that will satisfy him. He can't be convinced that everything will be all right, although having Wolfie to hold comforts him. Susan's daughter Dana figures out pretty quickly that, since she can't answer Wally's questions, she will divert him. *SpongeBob SquarePants* is showing on the TV, so Dana prompts Susan to ask Wally about this character, "who lives in a pineapple under the sea" and has friends like Patrick the starfish and Sandy the squirrel. In the end, Wally comes back to his questions, and the one he keeps asking over and over: "Is my dad dead? Is my dad dead?"

Susan says no each time and hopes she is telling the truth.

As it gets later, Susan and Dana decide to spend the night in Wally's room. They will stay until Arthur's parents arrive tomorrow. Wally is talking to Wolfie about what happened. Susan settles into a chair, and Dana curls up in the hospital bed with Wally, who says his broken leg is starting to hurt more.

About one o'clock in the morning, a doctor comes to find Susan to report on Arthur's latest surgery. In addition to internal injuries, Arthur has multiple breaks in all his limbs; the orthopedists are working to stabilize his legs and arms. St. Charles is a trauma hospital, and the physicians are used to challenging cases; however, because Arthur has so many things wrong with him, all the doctor can tell Susan is that Arthur came through the surgery, that he will remain in the Critical Care Unit for quite a while, and it is impossible to tell if he will survive.

Four hours later, a nurse comes in to ask Susan if she will come to my room in Critical Care. The nurse tells her that my blood pressure and pulse are really high and because of that they want to lower my medication, but they think I need someone familiar to talk to me, so I will calm down. Even though I am unconscious, I am agitated.

Susan leaves Dana with Wally and goes down to CCU. When she gets to my bed, she sees a bolt of metal sticking out one side of my head, just above the forehead; she sees a swollen face without discernible angles; she sees stitches and dried blood. She doesn't know what to say. She thinks that talking about the mundane, the daily, will be most reassuring, so she starts in about her job, her family, the play her older daughter is in, Sunriver, anything just to keep the words flowing. And as she speaks, she watches the monitors, and she can see the levels going down, my blood pressure beginning to stabilize. She sits there talking for hours. Every once in a while, she tries to get my attention.

"Nancy, can you hear me? It's Susan. Can you hear me?"

She keeps at it, sprinkling her stories with the repeated question: "Nancy, can you hear me? It's Susan."

At first I can't see more than a little gray light. I feel like a cotton plant — a long, dried-out stick with bolls of cotton weighing me down. Heavy. I have no notion of time passing. I feel as if I am asleep under a deep, cottony blanket.

"Nancy, it's Susan. Can you hear me?"

The woman is persistent, but I want to stay where I am.

"Nancy, there's a doctor here who wants to ask you some questions."

I want both of them to go away. No questions.

"Ms. Johnson, can you tell me what year it is?" A male voice through the heavy cotton and gray light.

"Nineteen ninety-four," I say.

"Do you know what month it is?" he asks.

"Um, December."

"Can you tell me where you live?"

"Washington, D.C?"

"Do you know where you are?"

"No."

"You and Arthur and Wally were in a terrible car accident, and you're all in the hospital," Susan tells me.

The blanket folds over me more deeply. I can tell there is activity around me, but I can't locate it. I am not uncomfortable, and I have no reaction to Susan's news.

## WHAT ELSE IS GOING ON

Now it's time to talk about what else is going on — and to talk about what our narrator can't, because she doesn't know from her own experience, because no one has told her, or maybe because some events are just too difficult for her to discuss with strangers. And since she is human, we have to allow that she sometimes gets things wrong.

Life happens in layers. The surface is easy; it's those layers under the surface where mystery resides. This is the unspoken territory, where the characters live as children, where the unconscious is busy all of the time with no sense of time, where dreams are manufactured and sought or lost. This is fire in the marsh grass, purple martins zooming in and out of bird hotels, silence interrupting conversation.

For starters, let's make some changes. In my part, I will change our narrator's name from Nancy. The name was given to her by someone who hated her, and the author herself has never liked it. She would like to be called Dervs, so that's what we will call her. A man who loved her named her Dervs, and it still sounds good to her even though he died some years ago, days before his thirty-second birthday. In some way, the name brings him into the present for her, gives her somebody reliable to talk to.

We are going to leave Dervs with Susan for now and go back to Wally's room, where he is lying in bed

14

with Wolfie and Dana. Wally's leg hurts, and his back hurts too. In his mind, he is still lying on the side of the road, feeling those prickles and thistles and rocks under him, with all the dust in the air making it hard to breathe, all the dust sticking in his lungs. And so much noise: the crash louder than anything in the world, a man shouting at him to unlock the car door, sirens, horns, yelling, Mom crying with all that blood on her face, and Dad not making any sounds at all.

Wally wants Wolfie to talk to him, but Mom makes Wolfie talk and Wally doesn't know where she is. Mom puts her hand in Wolfie's pocket — his puppet opening — and makes his head move when he talks. Sometimes even his ears move to show that he is listening. Wolfie's best friend, Big Bear, talks too, but Big Bear is at home and Wally misses him. Wolfie talks in a high voice, but Big Bear's voice is low and heavy. Big Bear is really solid, and Wally wants him here right now. Wally wants him to say that Daddy isn't dead.

Wolfie is about a foot tall with a tail nearly as long as his body. Arthur bought him at Wolf Trap, when he and Dervs were just married and they'd gone there to hear James Brown. When Arthur gave Dervs this wolf puppet, she thought it was cute but weird. She had no need for or love of puppets. But in the way that time slides, it may have been sliding for Arthur that night. He may have known, standing in an outdoor theater in Virginia, that ten years later his son was going to need this toy animal.

Wally was the one who chose Wolfie from the

start. Dervs used to make the wolf talk to Wally from the time he was an infant. It was Wolfie who Wally wanted to hold when he went to sleep as a toddler, and then Wolfie who went to school with him on the first day. Wolfie, with Dervs's hand in his pocket, helped Wally talk out his problems. And here he was now, rescued, and keeping Wally company when no one else could and when all Wally kept seeing was his mother's bloody face.

And while he was seeing her face, she was focused on him too. Those questions the doctor asked Dervs — where was she, what month and year it was — her answers put her at the time of Wally's birth, December 1994 in Washington, D.C., where they used to live. She was with her son, even though he didn't know it.

Jeff Foote arrives at St. Charles about nine o'clock in the morning, having driven down from Portland. He stops in to check up on Arthur first and is told the same thing Susan heard: it is impossible to tell if he will survive. Jeff has already called other friends of Arthur's from Oregon and Washington states, and some of them are on their way to the hospital. After seeing Arthur, Jeff crosses the Critical Care Unit to see Susan and me. He and Susan agree that he will stay with me a while, so she can look in on Wally and Dana and possibly get a little sleep.

I hear a different voice — "Nancy, it's Jeff. Can you hear me?" — and think I see a face in front of me, blurry, maybe five inches from my face.

"Nancy, you and Arthur and Wally were in a bad traffic accident yesterday, and you are all in a hospital in Oregon. Do you remember anything about that?"

I don't remember anything. I need to go back to sleep. I want the blanket back, to crawl under it, to feel the comfort of its cottony self.

Jeff stays with me for hours, talking about random events in his life, calling up stories and events I won't remember.

Later in the morning, another doctor comes in and asks if I know what year it is.

"Two thousand two," I say.

"What month is it?"

"September?"

"Close enough. Do you know where you live?"

"Oakland, California."

He asks me to stick out my tongue. I can do that. I think it's important. I stick out my tongue in what I believe is a forceful, I-mean-business way. This seems crucial, this business of sticking out my tongue.

"All right," the doctor says. "Let's get the bolt out."

Somehow I know the bolt is in my head, but I'm not sure how I know that. And right away I'm floating down again. Whatever is in or out of my head doesn't concern me. I just want the cushion of sleep.

I wake a little, just enough to hear Susan asking me if there is anyone I want to come.

"Ann," I say, meaning Ann Cummins, my close friend.

I feel as if my head is filled with the cotton balls now, like white dryness is taking up all the space; I can't think. The inside of my skull feels swathed in cotton, the blanket has moved from my exterior to the interior. I can't locate myself in time or space. Free-floating is what I am, with faces moving in front of me. I am reminded of those floating heads in horror movies, translucent ghost heads detached from their bodies.

Jeff and Susan and some faces I don't recognize appear from time to time. I'm doing okay, and now Susan is talking to me again, demanding my attention. She's telling me that Wally needs to have an operation on his leg, but he's afraid to have the anesthesia because he doesn't know what will happen. He doesn't want the doctors putting him to sleep. Can I talk to him on the phone to tell him to do it? Can I let him know I am all right and that he will be all right?

"Okay," I say.

I trust Susan, I know that much, and the mention of Wally has given me some energy or coherence, even though I have no idea what's going on.

*I can do this. What is it I'm doing?*

Susan has called Wally's room and hands me the telephone.

I hear my son's seven-year-old voice. "Mom? Are you okay?" I can feel his fear traveling through the phone line. His voice is immediate, the only thing I can hold in my head.

"Hi, Honey. I'm okay," I say. "Are you all right?"

"Mom, they want to put me to sleep to fix my leg. It really hurts, but I don't want to have an operation."

"Listen, Wally. The doctor is going to fix your leg so it won't bother you, but he can't do it while you are awake because that will hurt too much. Let them do it. Nothing bad is going to happen."

"I don't want them to put me to sleep."

"You won't even know you're going to sleep. You just count backward, and when you wake up, your leg will feel much better. I love you. This is going to be just fine. Can you do this?"

*Am I doing okay? I'm not even sure what I'm saying. Am I telling him the truth?*

"I guess so. Mom, where are you?"

"I'm in the hospital, Wally, but I'm not sure where.

You are going to be all right, Honey."

"Mom? Is Dad dead?"

He asks this, and it occurs to me that I don't know.

"No," I tell him. "He's just in another part of the hospital."

"Have you seen him, Mom?"

"No, Sweetie, I haven't seen him. After you finish this operation and feel better, we'll go see him together. Okay?"

"Okay."

"I love you, Honey. You're going to be fine."

"I love you too, Mom."

I'm exhausted by this conversation. I have no thoughts about it, and don't know how the phone gets hung up. I have to go back to sleep.

When I wake up, I see Marcia, my mother-in-law. She must have come in from Pennsylvania. I ask her what's going on. She tells me about the accident and says that Al, Arthur's father, is with Arthur, who is very seriously injured. I'm still trying to make sense of this, fighting my way through a forest of this damned cotton stuff in my head. I can't seem to conjure a clear thought or response to anything.

A little while later, Susan comes in and tells me that Ann is coming and will be here in Oregon tomorrow. As soon as she gets the words out, I throw up, yellow liquid, all over her and the bedcovers. I have no control over this yellow goop coming out of me.

*Where are Wally and Arthur? Where the hell is Arthur?*

Wally is having his leg surgery, and Marcia has told me that Al will be staying in the hospital room with him overnight. Wally's tibia was broken in such a way that it is taking some time and skill to set. He will be in an ankle-to-thigh cast for a month.

Marcia is talking, and I'm trying to grasp words, ideas. She says she and Al flew in this morning and are staying at the Ronald McDonald House, a block away from the medical center. I see colors in her words; the colors are coming through more clearly than the words and what the words mean. Marcia's eyes are bright green, and I try to center on them, to focus. At some point, she tells me that Wally came through the operation fine and that he will be released from the hospital tomorrow. They will all stay together at the Ronald McDonald House, so Wally can be close to Arthur and me.

*Where is Arthur? What is she talking about?*

"What about Wally's CF?" I ask. "Does the hospital know what's going on?"

"Yes, Honey. Dad and I called them on the phone Tuesday night, as soon as we realized it would be a problem."

Wally has cystic fibrosis. His doctor says that he has a mild case, but this is a chronic disease that destroys the lungs, so we are fanatic about doing everything we can to keep it at bay. So far, this approach has worked; Wally's lungs are functioning at one hundred percent. To stay that way, he puffs Albuterol through a gadget called a spacer twice a day, inhales Pulmozyme through a nebulizer once a day for seven minutes, and hooks himself up to a respiratory vest two times daily for fifteen minutes each. The vest is attached by hoses to a compressor. When he turns it on, the vest fills with air and then starts to jiggle. The purpose of this is to move around the mucous in Wally's lungs, so it's not such a good breeding ground for destructive bacteria and so he can cough it out. CF patients have thick, sticky mucous in their lungs, which bacteria love. You have to get things hopping around in there.

Since Wally's diagnosis two years ago, I have learned that cystic fibrosis is a disease about salt and its movement through the body. In CF patients the salt-to-water ratio is higher than it is in most people. This results in mucous that sometimes lodges where it shouldn't, for example, in the duct between the pancreas and the stomach where pancreatic enzymes normally flow. These enzymes make it possible for most people to digest fat and use it in our bodies. In CF patients this duct is clogged with mucous, so they have to get pancreatic enzymes in the form of capsules.

Other than maybe noticing that Wally takes pills — substitute pancreatic enzymes — when he eats, you wouldn't know to look at him that he has a disease. It doesn't affect his activity level or the way he appears. He comes in at about the fortieth percentile for height and weight, and at the top of the scale for energy.

"Don't worry," says Marcia. "Dad and I made sure we got a vest from the local cystic fibrosis chapter, and we got copies of Wally's prescriptions and had them filled, so we can make sure he does his treatments every day. It's a good thing you were with us earlier this summer, so we are on top of what he needs to do."

Relief seeps into me as I absorb this information.

I wake up in a room, an actual place I can see. I can locate myself in a bed and look out a window to my right. I see the sun shining on trees, think of Yeats's "birds in the trees" — from the opening of "Sailing to Byzantium" — and then the line a few stanzas down, "Once out of nature I shall never take / My bodily form from any natural thing." I can't get a grasp on my bodily form, but I love Yeats. If I could have chosen a name for myself, it would have been Maud Gonne, the name of the woman Yeats loved, his muse, to whom he proposed time after time and was always rejected. Maybe I'd change the spelling to Maude Gunn.

A nurse comes in and asks me how I feel and whether I can eat something. What would I like to eat, she wants to know.

"Anything?" I ask.

"Pretty much. We have a really good cafeteria," she says, "and patients can order anything, anytime they want. What would taste good to you? We have great milkshakes."

"A strawberry milkshake," I say, "and fruit salad." I crave something cold and sweet that takes no effort.

Marcia is with me. She says they moved me out of Critical Care and into this private room on the fourth floor this morning, and that Ann will be arriving soon.

She also tells me that Susan and Dana went back home to Ashland.

I don't remember moving rooms.

*How did I get moved? Did Susan come in to say goodbye?*

"How is Arthur?" I ask Marcia.

"Well, Honey, he's holding his own. He has some serious injuries."

She fiddles with her scarf as she talks, fingering green and blue silk roses.

"But he's going to live, isn't he?"

"We don't know."

*She doesn't know? How can she not know?*

No wonder she's fiddling. I can't get my head around this.

"When can I see him?"

"You aren't allowed to get out of bed yet. You've had a lot of injuries too. You may not realize that, but you've got to be careful for a while. I think you lost a lot of blood."

"How's Wally? I need to see Wally."

"You can't see Wally just yet. We can talk about that later."

"No, I need to see Wally. Where is he? What happened to me?"

Marcia tells me that I have a traumatic head injury and have been in and out of consciousness for the two days since the accident. I don't know what a traumatic head injury is. She also tells me I have some bad facial cuts. I raise my right arm enough to get my hand up to feel my face, just touch it lightly. Now that I think about it, my face feels masky, as if there is a thin layer of clay hardening all over it.

"Be careful," Marcia says.

I feel a gash and stitches going from the top left of my forehead down through my left eyelid, ending at the lashes. It's swollen. I can't close my left eye, but I didn't realize that until this moment. I feel another long gash across my neck, running from the left side to the middle. I try to raise my left arm, because there is something going on around my left ear — I think the hair around my ear has been shaved off — but my arm hurts. When I look, I see that my forearm is wrapped in bandages. I look at Marcia.

"You had to have surgery for that too; they got in an arm specialist," she says. "They told us your arm was sliced down to the bone, and there was a chance you might lose the movement in your hand. I think you had some good surgeons."

*When did all this happen? Did all this happen in two days? How long have I really been here?*

I wiggle the fingers of my left hand. They seem stiff but fine. I pull the covers off and look at the quilt-like stitch patterns going down my left leg. There are stitches and bandages all over the place and what looks like a giant dent on my left thigh.

"What's the big dent?" I ask, putting my hand into the depression on my leg. I run my hand back and forth through the thigh valley.

"I don't know. You'll have to ask the doctor."

I'm tired again. This information is making me tired. I can't focus.

When I wake up, Marcia is still sitting next to me.

"How did you get here?" I ask.

"We flew in Wednesday morning. That was yesterday."

"How did you know about the accident?"

"It was the strangest thing. We were in the car, driving from Philadelphia home to Harrisburg, when the car phone rang. Al and I looked at each other because nobody has the car phone number. He picked up the phone and put it on speaker. This voice on the other end — "

Before she can get out the next word, Al himself walks into the room, big smile on his face.

"You're looking more alert, Sweetie," he says.

*How could I be looking more alert? I don't remember having seen him before this.*

"Have you been with Arthur?" I ask. "How's Arthur?"

"He's holding his own. He has a lot of broken bones and he's had a bad brain trauma and he was having trouble breathing. I think he had a collapsed lung, so he's got tubes in his lungs, internal injuries, and I don't even know what else. But he's holding his own."

*Holding his own. What does that mean? Holding his own what?*

"When can I see him?"

"The doctors say you can't get out of bed, but I'll stay there with him, so he's not alone. I just wanted to come by and say hello to you. I know Ann's coming today. That will be good."

"I need to see Wally," I say. "When can I see Wally?"

"We don't think you should see Wally yet," says Al.

He fleets a glance at Marcia.

"Why not?" I persist. "I need to see him. He needs to see me."

"Honey, I don't think you know what you look like," says Marcia. "Dad and I didn't even recognize you when we got here. They sent us to see you in Critical Care, and when we got there, we thought they had sent us to the wrong place. We went back to the nurse's station and told them it wasn't you, and they said yes, it was."

She tells me that my face is pretty swollen and cut up and that they talked to a social worker, who also thought it would be better for me to wait to see Wally.

"He's already been so traumatized," she adds.

"I *know* he's traumatized. That's why he needs to see me. I need to see him now."

"You're not supposed to get agitated, Nancy," says Al.

"I am agitated, and I'm going to get more agitated if I don't see Wally. He needs to see me."

They look at each other and nod, then Marcia says, "Okay. I'll go get him but, Honey, you need to know he's in a wheelchair."

"I'm going to go check on Arthur and come back in a little while," says Al, as he and Marcia scuttle towards the door.

I don't know how long I'm asleep this time, but I'm slouching up in bed when I hear a commotion. First I see a foot and plaster-casted, bent-at-the-knee leg come through the doorway, then a chair with a boy in it, and then the boy's face with the biggest smile I have ever seen. No one has ever been this happy to see me. I start to cry.

Wally looks at me with that smile and says, "Oh, Mom, you look so much better than the last time I saw you. You look great!"

He looks great. He's wearing a yellow t-shirt with a picture of a wolf on it and a pair of gray shorts and already has signatures on his cast.

"Come over here with that chair," I say, and Marcia wheels him over to the bed.

Neither of us can move enough to get in a good hug, but we're touching; we can feel the solidness, the reality of each other. It's as if a tangible, collective cloud of fear has risen out of us and is dissipating in the air.

"How are you?" I ask.

"My leg hurts, Mom, but it's better."

"I know I look bad, Wally, but my face will heal."

"Mom, you look so much better than you did in the accident. When the car stopped bouncing, you turned around to look at me. I never saw anything like it. Your face was just blood. There was all this blood dripping off and then you started screaming. It was gross, and I couldn't stop thinking about it all night."

"I am so sorry you had to see that. But you can see I'm okay now, right?"

"Yep. Where's Dad? I want to see him. I thought he was dead."

"Daddy's in another part of the hospital. As soon as

they let me get up, we'll go see him together. Okay?"

"Okay."

Al and Marcia are both standing behind Wally. Al looks at me and mouths, "You were right. I'm sorry."

The visit is short. Marcia is taking Wally to physical therapy, so he can learn how to walk on crutches. I lie back and think about getting to see Arthur. I'm drifting off when the phone next to the bed rings. It takes me a couple seconds to figure out what's going on, and then I stretch out my right arm to see if I can reach it.

"Hello," I say.

There is silence on the other end. Then a familiar voice says, "Nancela, is that you? Is that you?"

It's Arthur's sister, Rikki, and she's sobbing into the phone.

"Rikki?"

"You sound just like yourself," she says. "I didn't imagine you would answer the phone; I was hoping to find my dad. I'm so relieved that you sound like yourself. I didn't know what to expect."

Rikki lives in San Francisco and tells me that she wants to come up to the hospital, but that Al has told her to stay home. She wants to know, do I think she should come? How is Pip doing? Pip is her family's nickname for Arthur.

I don't know, I tell her. I don't know how he's doing because I haven't been able to see him. All I've been told is they're not sure he's going to live. Even as I'm saying this, I know something's not right; I'm saying these words, but I have no feelings to go along with them. Rikki is crying, and I'm just saying words.

Finally, I say to her, "You need to come. Your brother needs you."

Rikki is five years younger than Arthur, and the two of them have been close their whole lives. Maybe she can do something to help him. I don't know what I'm doing, but I figure the more people here for Arthur the better.

"Thank you," she says. "I'll be there Saturday. I need a day to get things organized for the kids before I leave."

*What day is today?*

Sometime in the afternoon, a familiar face pokes her head through the door — my friend Ann. She comes in and sits next to me. She tells me I look good. She talks about the university where she teaches, her musician husband, Steve, the rental car she has, and she makes me feel better. I have lost touch with life, and she is bringing it into the room. She has also brought me a bracelet, for healing, she says. It's a thick silver strand curling around a lapis, made by a Native American artist. Ann grew up on the Navajo Reservation, and I credit her with knowing about healing. She tells me this lapis is for healing.

She stays while I eat a veggie burger and have a straw-berry milkshake. She stays while nurses come in and take readings, my vitals, they say. I ask Ann if she can find a mirror, so I can look at my face. Okay, she says, and finds one. Maybe it's the brain injury, or maybe I expected something worse, but when I look in the mirror, I see that I still have my teeth and that is reassuring. My hair is matted and clumped with blood, prickly. I don't like it so much. I touch it. Sticky, it feels like it's full of little burrs. I think that's just the hair ends sticking up every which way from the blood, although maybe some of the roadway is in there too, some of the dust and stones.

My forehead looks a little like Frankenstein's monster. It is swollen and protruding about two inches beyond its normal size and there are black stitches going down it and on through my left eyelid. There isn't much skin on my left cheek — it's scraped and swollen, beginning to scab over — but the right side isn't so bad. There are some lumps in my right eyelid. The hair is shaved around my left ear. My ear itself looks fine, but a series of stitches winds around it. My neck takes me back to the monster; the stitches in my neck remind me of the stitches where his head was attached. I imagine Gene Wilder as my surgeon, Igor saying, "What hump?"

"You're right," I say to Ann. "I don't look so bad. I would recognize me."

Christian Friesse comes in early in the morning and wakes me. He introduces himself as an ear-nose-throat specialist and tells me he wants to talk about my face. He says I have a blowout fracture. This is no shock to me; my entire world has been blown out, why not my face? Sometimes vocabulary fits the event.

As he describes it, the orbit bone around my left eye has been broken and with it the sinus bones. These are thin and fragile and when smashed, they fall as broken potato chips. He says I'm lucky I didn't lose my eye. He wants to operate, to take the septum from my nose and plant it under my eye to replace the bottom of the orbit bone. He will go in through my lower lid, and says the scar shouldn't be noticeable.

"Removing the septum isn't a problem?" I ask.

"No, in fact, some people say they have fewer sinus problems after this kind of an operation."

*How many people have this kind of an operation?*

"When do you want to do this?" I ask him.

He is going away for a week on Sunday, to the San Juan islands, so is hoping to do the surgery early tomorrow. Then he'll take the stitches out when he gets back.

"I need you to sign a release form for me to do it," he says.

"Okay," I say, and sign.

If you ask me what the release form says, I don't know.

33

If you ask me to describe the man who will be cutting into my face, I can't. I don't register how people look so much as I try to stick with what they say, how voices sound, how consonants move around vowels. Someone said I was in shock. What is shock, anyway, except the body's immediate reaction to trauma? *Shock, shock, shock.* I say it and all those Ks go knocking together. How long does shock last?

I'm sitting with Ann, chomping down yet another veggie burger, when I hear noises in the hall. I look up to see my stepbrother, John, and his wife, Chris, walk into the room.

"Hey, you guys," I mumble, through the vegetable mash.

I watch John's face redden and twizzle; I think he's going to cry. I'm wondering how they got here from Pennsylvania and at the same time am really happy they did, when John says, "I never thought I'd see you look like this."

"I never thought I'd see you here," I quip. "How did you find out about this? When did you get in?"

Chris explains that this has been a difficult time for them, in part because the stories my family was getting at their home in Bethlehem were confusing and frightening. The first night they were told, "They both have bolts in their heads, intracranial pressure monitors." After the first day, she says it was clear I was going to get better, but there was nothing but bad news about Arthur. The best anyone would say was, "He's holding his own."

John and Chris want to see Arthur. So do I. I call for a nurse and ask if I can do that. She says I can get out of bed and go down to see him if I feel all right. She's going to get me into a wheelchair first, and then, if I feel well enough, she'll try to fix up my hair, get some of the blood out, and we can go down to CCU. I am excited; I can tell that, but I'm having trouble coming up with other emotions. I want to see Arthur. The rest I can't figure out or have no words for.

After I am up and in the wheelchair and I feel okay, there is a sudden flurry of activity, although I can't focus on who is doing what. I'm being pushed through beige hallways, into an elevator, and then into a warren of rooms that is the Critical Care Unit. I am wheeled through a doorway and then boom — in front of me is my husband. He is somewhere in there among the equipment and bandages and casts, tubes leading in, wires leading out. His chest is bare, adorned with the tubes and wires; a huge purple welt diagonally bisects his chest and abdomen. I look for his face. He's so pale. I want to see his eyes, but only his right eye is open.

This is where the music should rise and violins come in and I should rush to his side in a moment of great passion, but I hear only beeps and burrs from the army of machines. I feel a constriction in my chest. Otherwise, nothing.

"Arthur," I say. "Arthur, it's me."

"Hi, Honey," he says, as if I had walked out of the room five minutes ago to get a drink of water.

Al is here, telling me that Arthur can talk, but his brain injury may mean he won't make sense. Everyone is relieved that he recognizes my voice. Someone maneuvers my wheelchair so I'm next to his right side, but it's impossible to get too close because of all the monitors. Al tells me to talk to Arthur, so I do. I tell him I'm doing okay, that Wally is fine, has a broken leg. Arthur is smiling and turns his head toward me, but I can't tell what he sees. He seems to recognize me, but he starts talking about being in Philadelphia.

Arthur's head injury is the sort in which he can't really locate the present, so he lives in different layers of time. When he is in Philadelphia, where he had his first job as a lawyer, everything he says is true about his time there. He is talking to people who were in his life then, the places are real, and he thinks he is whatever age he was when he lived there. But his time frame changes quickly. One minute he's twenty-five years old in Philadelphia, the next he's thirty-five in Washington, D.C., running a meeting at his law firm. The only place he isn't is here, in this present.

Now Arthur is yelling, "Take the pants! Take the pants! Take the shoes!"

I don't know what's happening in his brain.

"How soon will he come out of this?" I ask a doctor who has come into the room.

"We have no way to know that. Generally, we hope that patients come out quickly. They seem to have a greater chance of recovering if they do."

"Can you give us a time frame for what to expect?" asks Al.

"I can't really," the doctor says. "We just hope it will be soon."

Now Al can't stop himself from talking, and more words spill out of him.

"Well, what's the worst case we could expect?"

*Stop talking, Al! Why are you asking this? Get off this fucking train!*

The doctor looks at Al and says, "The worst case is, he may never recover."

*Al, you stupid shit! Why did you want those words to come out?*

John has, meanwhile, gone outside and is talking to one of the nurses. He is asking her about Arthur's injuries, if she will write them down for him, so he has something to show our family in Bethlehem rather than try to remember everything. When he pushes her for a prognosis, all she says is that it doesn't look good. A year later, Chris will give me the nurse's injury list:

> *Brain injury* — small hemorrhagic contusion
>     (bruise on the right side of his brain), small
>     hemorrhage in the occipital horn of the right
>     lateral ventricle (one of the chambers in the
>     right brain)
> *Bilateral pulmonary contusions* — bruising to
>     both lungs
> *Bilateral pneumothoraces* — air between the lung
>     tissue and the lung sacs that shouldn't be there
>     (that's what the chest tubes are for)
> *Small laceration of spleen*
> *Right renal contusion* — bruised kidney

*Multiple left rib fractures* — broken ribs
*Transverse lumbar fracture*
*Bilateral tibia/fibula fractures* — lower leg bones
    broken, both legs
*Left radius/ulna fracture* — both bones in left
    forearm broken
*Right wrist fractures* — multiple right hand and
    wrist bones broken
*Left femur fracture* — thigh bone broken
*IVC filter has been placed* — inferior vena cava
    filter to reduce risk of pulmonary embolism

I am back in my room, flipping through a *Vogue* magazine Ann has brought me — diversion, she said — when Marcia comes in to tell me she has my wallet.

"My wallet?"

"Yes, somebody found it at the accident scene, and they had your and Pip's wallets locked up here for safekeeping. The social worker told me about it, and I got them back for you."

"Thank you. Can I have it?"

"You want it now?"

"Yes," I say. "Where is it?"

"I have it back at the Ronald McDonald House," says Marcia. "You shouldn't have it in your hospital room. I can keep it until you get out of the hospital."

"No, I need my wallet."

"But Nancy, you can't really keep it here. Anybody could walk in and take it. Why do you want it?"

"Because it has all my ID in it. I'm alone in here. If I

don't have it with me, nobody will know who I am."

"Okay," she says. "I'll bring it next time I come."

She looks out the window.

"Listen," she says after a long moment. "I should tell you that Wally's been having terrible nightmares. We have him sleeping in the same room as Dad and me, and he wakes up screaming several times a night. I'm not sure what to do about it. I can't tell what will make him feel better. Do you have any suggestions?"

"What will make him feel better is for me to get out of here," I say.

"I know that, but it's way too early for you to think about that yet."

Later on Jeff stops by to say that he and some other of our friends have discussed what needs to be done, and he's offering to be our lawyer — to take care of any legal issues surrounding the accident and also to deal with insurance problems resulting from our medical bills — if I want him to. He offers to do this at no cost. The attorneys think we need to have someone representing us just in case anything comes up, particularly with insurance companies. Apparently, there are a number of Arthur's lawyer friends here. I only remember Jeff and another friend, Mike, who, I think, was feeding me Jell-O at some point, but I could be making that up.

I don't know what legal problems we could have; I haven't thought about this for a second, but I'm grateful that someone, not me, will be dealing with them. I have no idea what will be chasing us, or what we will be chasing, for years. Jeff also tells me that he thinks it will be a good idea to set up an 800 number that people can call to get an update about our conditions. He tells me that the hospital and our family members are overwhelmed by the number of people calling to find out what's happening to us, particularly about Arthur's condition. Jeff says he will keep the 800 number updated daily, if I think it's a good idea. I think it's a good idea. Because of his work, Arthur has friends all over the country. He's an extrovert, externally driven — gregarious, entertaining, gaining energy from interaction. He's great on the telephone; after we started living together, he'd be on the phone with various friends from the time he got home from work until dinner. I finally asked him if he could cut down on the conversations. In the best of circumstances, I am adequate on the phone. I don't know what I would say now.

After everyone has left my room for the day, I eat fruit salad and drink another strawberry milkshake. I haven't had much pain; my whole body feels stiff, unfamiliar, but otherwise I'm pretty comfortable. They must be giving me something. Everyone at this hospital has been so nice. I want to stay here and have them take care of me for a long time. But I decide I have to leave as soon as I can convince them to release me. It's time to get back to the mom job.

## WITH REGARD TO YOUR SON

Isn't that the way? Just when things get comfortable, you have to leave. Dervs knew it would be hell out of her hospital bed, but they were all in hell — different versions, same psychic playing field. Al's may have been the worst — other than Arthur, who didn't know where he was, so maybe it doesn't matter about that. On the other hand, he has those memories somewhere, doesn't he?

But Al — Arthur's father — he was the one who thought he should fix things or change them, at least take care of everyone. When the car phone rang on that drive to Harrisburg Tuesday afternoon, he had no idea who was calling. He didn't even catch the name, just heard a male voice identify himself as a social worker.

"I'm trying to reach the father of Arthur Bryant," the voice said.

"This is Al Bryant. I'm Arthur's father."

"Sir, I'm calling from St. Charles Medical Center in Bend, Oregon. I'm sorry to have to tell you this, sir, but your son and his family have been involved in a terrible car accident. You might want to get here as soon as possible. Your son and his wife are both in serious condition."

"When you say soon, what do you mean? Are you telling me they could die?"

Silence on the other end and then, "With regard

41

to your son, sir, yes, within the next twenty-four hours."

Al had been a fighter pilot during World War II, and the adrenaline response that kept him in the air then kicked in now, as if half a century hadn't passed. He told Marcia to write down the contact information and said they would make arrangements to be at the hospital no later than the following morning. Neither he nor Marcia spoke for the rest of the drive. Nothing in his head. There was nothing in his head except for shortening the length of road between him and home and *please, God, don't let him die*. Al needed to get home, so he could get to Pip.

Here it was: the man and his son. On the wall of his office, Al had hung a drawing of a man holding his young son's hand. You could see them from the back, the two of them walking off toward the future together. Arthur had that picture in *his* office now, the only thing he'd wanted when his father retired and closed his construction firm. Al, the acoustical contractor, whose son went to Swarthmore and Harvard, whose son headed a public interest law firm, whose son was out there fighting to make the world better, whose son had never disappointed him. Here was Al being told that his son could be dead before Al could reach him.

Al focused on one thing and then the next: getting home, making flight reservations, calling Arthur's mother and his sisters and Dervs's family, arranging to have the mail taken in, getting a ride to the airport.

42

All the while praying for Arthur to stay alive. Marcia packed while Al made arrangements. They tried to sleep, couldn't, stayed up all night until it was time to leave.

Marcia was Al's third wife. His first was Marjorie, Arthur's mother. Her picture was painted on the side of his plane during the war. He and Marjorie had four children together — three girls and a boy. Not a good match, they were going to separate when Arthur was in high school. But Marjorie contracted the Hong Kong flu and then meningitis and encephalitis. Al stayed in the marriage another five years. After her illness, Marjorie was told she would never walk again; she couldn't accept that and made herself relearn it all. She could walk now, but not fluidly, and she couldn't travel without assistance. Al told her he would let her know what was happening to Arthur as soon as he knew.

Al's job was to keep it together for everybody. He told the girls, Arthur's three sisters, to stay home. And they listened to him, at least Rikki did until she talked to Dervs. Al didn't want any of them to have to deal with the immediacy of Arthur's death. He was protecting them, doing his job.

That was why he didn't want Wally to see Dervs; he was trying to protect his grandson. You can let Dervs be mad at him for that, but don't you be. In these circumstances, everyone is crazy, and they are each doing the best they can.

At the hospital, Al tried to manage the doctors,

the lawyers, the friends and family members. The surface of his mind was busy with arrangements, filling up the space as fast as it could with the next task and the next one. On the second level, he was praying, talking to Arthur, holding Arthur's hand, cajoling him to come back, telling his son he couldn't leave his family, his work, all the people who needed him.

But down there deeper in his mind, Al called on all the barriers he could. He worked harder than he ever had to keep knowledge out. The man who prided himself on knowing things tried his best not to know this: how the world feels when your child has left it, how it feels when you have failed to protect him.

When I wake up, a nursing assistant is taking my vital signs. I ask her when my eye surgery is scheduled.

"Oh, they did that early this morning. Don't you remember?"

*No. I have no memory of that.*

I feel my face. There isn't even a bandage.

She tells me to be careful not to touch my eye, gives me a mirror so I can see where the stitches are.

My face is still swollen and scabby, but I don't see any evidence of part of my nose having moved to under my eye.

"I can't see anything," I say.

"Dr. Friesse is good; he's the one you want working on your face. Here, see these tiny stitches just under your left eye? That's where he went in."

I can barely see the stitches.

I call the Ronald McDonald House to ask John if he and Chris will bring Wally over so he can see Arthur. They arrive within the half hour. I have proven to the nurses that I am all right to walk and have put on a second hospital gown, so my butt doesn't stick out. John pushes Wally's wheelchair, and we make our way down to the CCU. On the way, I talk to Wally about Arthur's head injury.

"Daddy may not recognize you," I tell him, "but it's not because he doesn't want to. He had a terrible bump to his head, and his brain isn't functioning the way it usually does. Can you handle it if he isn't able to talk to you?"

"I can handle it, Mom. I just want to see Dad."

I am afraid. I don't know how this child will be able to deal with the way Arthur looks, laid out with all the tubes and monitors.

We walk into the room. Arthur looks the same to me.

"Hey, Arthur. I don't know if you can see him, but Wally is here in his wheelchair to visit you," I say. "He's in a wheelchair because he has a broken leg, but don't worry; otherwise, he is all right."

"Hi, Daddy," Wally says.

His eyes are wide. His yellow shirt glows under the fluorescent lights.

Arthur breaks into a huge smile. He manages to turn his head toward us and says, "Hey, Wallster."

Then he tries to raise his right arm from the elbow in an attempt to give Wally a high five or maybe a thumbs up. His thumb is the only part of his wrist and hand not in a cast. Wally beams. We each talk to Arthur, mostly about the hospital and the Ronald McDonald House and who has been visiting. Arthur doesn't say anything else while we are there. But he gave us one moment, five seconds really, in which we all three were in the same place and time.

Back in my room, I ask the nurse if I can meet with someone who can arrange my release from the hospital. A couple hours later a doctor comes in and tells me it's too early for me to leave.

"I have to get out," I tell him. "My son is so trauma-tized he wakes up with nightmares every couple hours. He needs to be with me, particularly because we don't know what will happen to Arthur. If anything happens to his father, he needs to be with me."

He says they can't release me until someone from Occupational Therapy certifies that I am able to function on my own.

"How soon can you arrange for that?" I ask.

"This is a weekend, so it might take some work. I'll see if I can get someone to come in tomorrow. I under-stand why you want to get out, but I need to tell you I think it's too early. On the other hand, this is an extraor-dinary circumstance, and you are the only one who can know what's best for your son."

I thank him for helping me. I am so grateful for this hospital. It's small and personal, and the care has been wonderful. All I want to do is stay here and drink straw-berry milkshakes and let them take care of me.

"Ms. Johnson, are you awake? I'm from Occupational Therapy. I came in to see if you are well enough to be released today. Do you need a little time to get ready?"

I go to the bathroom, brush my teeth and then I walk down to the OT rooms with the therapist, wondering what this woman is going to make me do to prove I can function. Some of the tests are simple. I have to push, pull, move objects. Then I have to pick up a block from the floor. This is the hardest task so far. I get dizzy when I bend over, so I focus my entire body on not falling. Everything hurts. My head and left arm are throbbing. When I have to place the block from the floor high onto a shelf, I think I won't be able to do it. I ran a marathon two months ago, and this is taking more focus, is more painful and difficult. I keep hoping each task will be the last, but when I look at the clock again, it's only been ten minutes. I can't keep this up. Then the OT says to me, "I think you can manage outside the hospital. I'll sign the release, then get it to the doctor on duty."

Before I leave the hospital, I am given a list of what's happened to my body and its current condition. The list includes a closed head injury and concussion, left scalp hematoma, left orbital blowout fracture (requiring surgical reconstruction), left facial lacerations, right neck hematoma, a deep wound over left ulna (repaired surgically), abrasions over my left tibia. A note is also made of an apparent five-by-eight-centimeter ovarian cyst with a recommendation that it be checked with a pelvic ultrasound.

After I sign the appropriate papers, I call the Ronald McDonald House and tell Wally I'll be there soon and that he and I will have our own room. He is ecstatic: "Mom, I'm going to work hard to learn to use the crutches, so you won't have to wheel me around." As if I could.

Ann gets me organized; I put on clothes and a hat she retrieved from somewhere, and I roll out of the St. Charles Medical Center into the Oregon light. The Ronald McDonald House is a block away along a sloping, curled walkway. The air is warm, although I'm supposed to stay out of the sun and particularly keep sun off my face because of all the skin abrasions. Walking has become its own project; I am slow. As I move forward, I think about how often I've trashed McDonald's fast food; so self-righteous, and here I am, eagerly making my way toward a place represented by a clown in a red-striped shirt.

As soon as I get to the door, a smiling woman comes to open it. She introduces herself as the house manager and welcomes me. Al and Marcia emerge from what looks like a dining area, and through the lobby, I can see Wally in his wheelchair playing a board game with John. The lobby has an information desk on the right, a doorway straight ahead leading into the dining room, and a computer table on the left. I feel overwhelmed by the space.

All I want to do is sit down, try to figure out something, anything. I want something to be simple; I want something to make sense.

The manager gives me a tour of the house, which includes a huge kitchen, laundry room, and the common room — what I thought of as the dining area — which has eight sets of tables and chairs. Then she takes me to the back hall where there is a large aquarium, a small TV room, and the bedrooms. She leads me down the hall to the penultimate door on the left, across from Al and Marcia's room. She explains that, of course, Wally and I can stay here because Wally was injured and also has to be close to his father. Because there is only one other family staying at the time, she is also making rooms available to Al and Marcia and Rikki, although they will have to leave if the house is needed for sick children and their families. A rule stretch from the Ronald McDonald House; I am impressed. I have been lucky enough in my life to have avoided social services, but now I appear to be on the fast track to needing them.

Wally is hot on my heels in his wheelchair, examining our room, ready to move Wolfie and the rest of his belongings in. He wants to set up camp on the big window seat. Al and Marcia have managed to rent a vest, compressor, and nebulizer from the local Cystic Fibrosis Foundation chapter, and they suggest we keep the equipment in their room, so Marcia can continue to supervise Wally's breathing sessions. That's okay with me.

I realize that I don't even know what belongings we have. What was recovered from the accident site? How much was salvageable? Other than what I'm wearing, do I have any clothes? I ask Marcia. She tells me Susan retrieved a lot of our stuff. Marcia has washed all our clothes for us.

"Laundry," she says. "It's what I do when everything else is out of control."

Back in the common room, John answers more of my questions about what was left from our car. He has emptied most of the suitcases and cleaned them of debris; however, he holds up the backpack my laptop was in.

"I took out your computer and the cables," he says, "but I want to show you something. Come on outside."

I follow him out to the back where the dumpsters are. He walks away from me. "Watch," he says, and turns the backpack upside down. A hailstorm of glass shards falls out, followed by a cloud of brown dirt. I have no words for this action, only a thud in my stomach. The sound of the glass hitting the concrete sinks into me, dust fills my nose until I can't breathe. There are no diamonds in these shards, no beauty, no light reflection.

John looks at me.

"That's what it was all like. I thought you ought to see it."

My father-in-law has decided we should all go out for dinner tonight, as a kind of celebration. He wants to thank Ann and Chris and John for coming. They have to leave tomorrow to get back to work by Tuesday. I am reminded that tomorrow is Labor Day. Al also wants to celebrate my getting out of the hospital and Arthur's continued resilience. After five days, and against the odds, his son is still alive.

"I made a reservation at a place that is like Benihana's," Al says. "I know Wally likes to go there in Harrisburg, so I thought it would be a treat for him."

I give up on getting other clothes on; it's too much work negotiating bandages. And my hair isn't worth combing. I think I'm allowed to take a shower soon, but I can't remember grooming details right now. I'll have to ask someone at the medical center tomorrow. As Wally and I walk into the common room to meet up with everyone, I realize that we're going to have to go to the restaurant in a car. I hadn't thought about that. When I mention it, John says we should go with Chris and him. Apparently, this was arranged ahead of time. They must have already discussed *the car issue.*

Wally is trying out his crutches, so he won't have to mess with the wheelchair in the restaurant. He thinks he can manage them and is doing all right as he goes out the front door. Then he sees John's rental car waiting in the driveway.

"Mom!" he nearly screams, "I don't want to go. I'm not going in a car!"

"This will be fine, Wally," I tell him.

*What the hell am I talking about? This is terrifying. I don't want to go in a car either.*

"I'm going to sit right next to you in the backseat," I say. "We'll do this together. You know that Uncle John is a great driver. We have to get back in a car sometime; it might as well be now."

Wally finally agrees, and we get into the car. I have my arm around his shoulders. Chris turns around from the front passenger seat and talks nonstop, trying to distract us for the five-minute ride. When we get there Wally seems a little spunkier as he maneuvers his crutches up the slanted walkway to the entrance.

Al, Marcia, Rikki, and Ann have already arrived and are seated around a semi-circular table with a preparation area at the straight side where the chef intends to make his knives dance on the steel grill. Wally and I sit next to each other, his crutches leaning against the wall. Rikki tells me that she didn't want to come out for dinner because she thinks somebody should stay with Arthur, but her father convinced her we should take this opportunity to all be together, if only for an hour or so. I hope they serve wine and then realize that, because of my brain injury, I've been warned not to drink for six months.

*Shit. And I can't feel the left side of my face. I'm tired; I just want to go to sleep.*

We order and try to be cheerful, and for a while that works. Al keeps talking about how well Arthur is doing — the long pep talk, maybe more believable with an audience. We're all in it too, saying yes, Pip's doing great, what a trooper, somebody's certainly home in there. After soup, during salad, Rikki decides to call home to talk to her five-year-old son and eight-year-old daughter before they go to sleep for the night. She goes out in the hall and comes back five minutes later weeping. Her daughter has told Rikki that she doesn't love her children as much as she does Uncle Pippy, or else why would she stay away from them? This is the first time Rikki has ever been away from her children for more than a couple hours, certainly not overnight, certainly not for several overnights. Chris gets up and walks Rikki outside, where we can see them sitting on the curb together, Rikki's shoulders heaving up and down.

Our chef comes over to the table, introduces himself, and begins his preparations. He wipes down the grill and gets out a canister from which he squirts oil over the stainless steel surface. With a flourish, he flicks a match and the oil flames up, part of the spectacle.

Wally starts screaming.

"It's fire! The fire! Put out the fire! Mom! Put out the fire!"

He is wailing as everyone yells at the chef, a young man who has no idea what's going on, to squash the flames. I grab Wally and pull him to me to hold him. None of us had thought about Wally's experience in the burning car.

When each of us settles as much as we are able, I look at Arthur's father. He is staring into a spot straight ahead of him. All of our nerve endings are exposed, everyone's. We are stunned by ourselves and by what has been a foolish attempt at normalcy. We are so far outside that circle now, eccentrically spinning off into psychic landscapes we don't recognize, landscapes inhabited by broken children, meals of dust, fiery explosions, and unnamable winged monsters plucking at our eyes.

My friend Cherise arrived yesterday. Apparently she and Ann coordinated the hand off, so there would be someone here with me all the time. Ann takes me out for breakfast this morning before she flies back to Flagstaff, where she teaches at Northern Arizona University. We go to a crowded local restaurant, the Alpenglow. Ann tells me I look fine to be out and about; however, when the waiter, who looks like a young college student, stops at our table, she says, "Wow, what happened to you?"

"Car accident," I say.

"Looks like you were lucky to get out alive."

I am the hungry survivor, the one who eats fruit and eggs and pancakes with marionberry syrup. I am going to miss Ann. I would be happy to have breakfast with her every day.

And I am happy to have Cherise here. She's smart and funny and she makes me laugh. We met when I was a graduate student and her English professor at the University of Arizona. Her mother died near the end of the semester, and I had to give Cherise a make-up exam because she missed the scheduled one while she was at the funeral. After the exam, we started talking, walked around for a while and began a friendship that has traveled well through time and place. She is now finishing her PhD in Art History at Stanford University and living in Oakland with her boyfriend, Geoff, so I get to see her often.

Cherise is like an older sister to Wally; she has known him since he was an infant, and she and Wally seem to have a deep-down understanding of each other. The bonus is he listens to her without giving her a hard time. One of the first things she says is that she's going to take over Wally duty for a while, so Marcia can have some time off. Cherise is willing to have Wally get mad at her if she pushes him about working with the crutches. Marcia is his grandma; no way she wants him angry.

Jeff Foote is back here in Bend, visiting Arthur, taking care of some business about the accident. Later today he's going to the junkyard where our car was towed. He's also going to talk to the police officers who were at the scene. I told him I want to go with him. He doesn't like the idea, but he said okay. I've discovered that an advantage to being injured is that it's easier to get my way, even if it doesn't seem to make sense. People will be here with Arthur and Wally. I want to do this. One of the three of us involved in the accident should have this information if only as part of our family's story. I should see the car, talk to the police. I spent nearly ten years as a journalist. I can do this, be useful.

Jeff picks me up in his black Escalade. I've never been in an SUV before.

"It's about the only car I can fit my frame in, and with all the driving I do, I want to be comfortable and safe," says Jeff, a lanky six feet seven or so, sandy hair, great smile.

He's easy to be with, and I think he must be really

tolerant to drag me along on this venture. He's been on this route before, so he knows where things happened. Unlike most of the days I've spent in Oregon this trip, today is cloudy, feels damp and chilling.

About half an hour out of Bend, Jeff says, "We're getting near the accident site. Do you want me to tell you where it is?"

I say yes, and ask if he can pull off the road when we get there. In a couple of minutes, he does so and parks the Escalade on the shoulder of Highway 97.

"Here it is," he tells me. "This driveway right in front of us belongs to Christopher Adney. This is what he was turning into when he hit you."

A hand-painted sign, red uppercase letters on a piece of plywood, at the front of the property advertises firewood for sale. The sign, riven and splintered, is propped up against some logs. A dirt driveway leads back to a house trailer, some junker cars. The air smells of pine trees and wood smoke. Everything but the trees is the color of sand. I look for thistles at the side of the road because Wally says the EMTs laid us on body boards where it was prickly. I look for skid marks. Jeff tells me there aren't any because Mr. Adney turned so quickly and without warning that Arthur never even had a chance to hit the brakes. I look at the dust on the side of the road, try to picture our bodies there, Arthur trapped, pissed-off people in their cars, honking, because the highway was closed for hours. So much activity, and now there is nothing. Not even in my memory.

I try to imagine what it sounded like, smelled like,

felt like, but I can't call up anything. It is as if I have never been here. I want to feel a connection to this place, even if what I feel is horrible, but I can't make it happen. I keep looking down Mr. Adney's driveway, thinking maybe he'll come out of his trailer and I can catch a glimpse of him. I want him to be scrawny and mangy, etiolated, skulking around his piece of dirt, eyes darting, looking for danger in the trees. Greasy hair, bad skin, afraid of shadows that have begun to haunt him, shadows that have emerged from my mind and the minds of all those people who love Arthur, all our nasty mind shadows tailing him — as long as he lives.

Neither Jeff nor I say anything as we start down the road again. In about fifteen minutes we see signs for Crescent Salvage, red rectangular signs, and then we pull off the road on the right, head down another winding dirt driveway, old cars, trucks, machinery on both sides of the road. We stop and Jeff points. It takes me about five seconds to register that at the end of his point is my car. It is nearly flat. As I walk over to it, I realize that it is no higher at its tallest point than my waist. I am five feet four. How tall does that make my car?

The remains of my silver Toyota station wagon are a collected jumble of metal and wire, not a discernible vehicle. There are no front doors, no windshields; almost everything has been crushed to the floor. Jeff tells me to look at the back windshield wiper, which is stretched and wrapped around the bottom of the car. Apparently this happened at the moment of impact, when the rear window blew out.

I look inside the car. We had been eating pretzels, drinking water, listening to music. There are bottles and pretzel crumbs all over, tennis balls, music tapes, Wally's green sunglasses. There is blood on the seats, the floor, the air bag. Arthur's ChapStick is stuck in what was the center console, and there is a flattened hubcap in the luggage area.

What takes my breath, makes my throat hurt again where the tubes were inserted, are Arthur's black jeans on the driver's side. One of his K-Swiss tennis shoes is there on the floor. The other is in the backseat. Now his earlier ramblings — "Take the pants! Take the shoes!" — make some kind of sense to me. He must have been trapped in such a way that both had to be removed to get him out of the car. Maybe he didn't want to go to the hospital without clothes, so he was telling the EMTs to take his pants with them. Or he was telling them they had to cut off his pants to free him. We may never know.

I look up from the car, making notes in my journal. I write down everything, now the number of our air bag: 930122G 0938. I see an old Chevy Silverado, its grill bashed in, the next row over.

"Is that Adney's truck?" I ask.

Jeff nods.

What's left of the brown and beige pickup is staring back at me — a one-eyed drunk with a twisted grin. I want to kill it.

As we get back into Jeff's car I am freezing, shaking. This, too, seems to be a result of my head injury — a broken thermostat. I have taken something for each of us from the car: Wally's sunglasses, dance tapes Arthur made, the shoes I was wearing — a pair of black-and-white Diesel slip-ons. This is the last time I will see this car. I want to remember it. Yesterday, a man stopped me in the hospital cafeteria. He recognized me from the accident, said he worked for AirLife, the organization that operates the helicopters that flew us from the crash scene to the hospital. He asked me about Arthur's status, nodded his head; he told me not to worry about what I looked like, that faces heal quickly. Then he said that he'd been doing his job for over twenty years and "had never seen a wreck like this with people alive."

Jeff and I drive out the rutted road to the highway and head north on our way to the police substation. At the small office, we are lucky enough to catch Trooper James Hayes, the first law enforcement officer to arrive at the scene of the accident. He's a young man with brown hair and an earnest, round face. He is surprised to see me. I tell him what's going on with Arthur and Wally and ask him for as many details as he can give me about the crash. He is the one who tells me about Mr. Carter, the man who pulled Wally out of the burning car.

I ask him about Mr. Adney. Trooper Hayes says that Adney was driving without a license — his having been suspended as a result of DUIs — and because he had no license, he had no insurance. Adney told him that he was coming from having breakfast at his girlfriend's house and had started to pass his driveway without noticing. That's why he made the fast turn. Trooper Hayes also tells me that Adney agreed to a Breathalyzer test for alcohol and that it was negative, but he refused to take a drug test, invoking his first amendment rights. The officer says, "That's what he said, that he was invoking his *first* amendment rights."

Trooper Hayes adds that they probably did a drug test at the hospital, where our Silverado driver was treated for bruises and released, and that information would be forthcoming. About Mr. Adney, he says, "He's going to do jail time for this." That is what I want to hear. I want him to serve big-time jail time.

On the way back to Bend, Jeff tells me there have been hundreds of people calling the 800 number to find out how we are. He says I can call anytime to listen to the messages people are leaving and that he will keep the tapes, so Arthur can listen to them when he gets better.
*That phrase — when Arthur gets better.*

Before John and Chris left on Monday, John told me he hated to go back to Pennsylvania because he couldn't see any improvement in Arthur and was still afraid he wouldn't make it. Fear of loss is in the air.

Two years from now, Chris will tell me that she remembers all of us sitting around the tables in the Ronald McDonald House the Sunday I got out of the hospital. She says they were shocked that I had been released. They didn't think I was in any condition to get out of the hospital, but I was adamant about taking care of Wally. She says she kept looking over at me, and it was as if my mind were trying to organize things, but she could tell it was just too much for me. She didn't think I had a true sense of what was going on, couldn't assimilate any of it, particularly how close to death Arthur was.

I focus on the quotidian, moving from one task to the next. The days are full of appointments with physicians, psychologists, social workers. At 10:30 this morning, I see Dr. Belza to have the stitches on my face, head, and neck removed. At 1:30, Dr. Villano takes out the stitches in my left arm. At 2:30, I take Wally to see Dr. Hoffman, a psychologist, for trauma counseling. At 4:30, I see her myself. We talk about head injuries, what to expect from myself, the best ways to deal with Arthur.

We have all been working hard to keep Arthur's room comfortable and familiar. I went out with Cherise yesterday and bought him a Hawaiian shirt to hang on the wall. Rikki collected some of his favorite music and bought a CD player to have in his room, to play quietly. We've put up photographs of family members, so he can look at faces he recognizes, or so he can remember our faces. Part of the problem is that we don't know what he knows. He is still playing the time game. He recognizes our voices, but they are never in the present time and place. We inhabit other scenes from his life, some real, others fantasized. He's holding a lot of meetings at his law firm, peopled by friends from all over the country, from all time periods.

I go in to see Arthur after my last appointment of the day and find a nurse talking to Rikki and Al, telling them that Arthur's lower right leg is badly infected and she will need to change the bandages as soon as she can gather enough medical personnel. She asks Rikki and me to help her out, so Arthur won't know anything is happening. As a result of the brain injury, he often doesn't register the pain that would normally be associated with his injuries. That will probably be the case with the bandage change, but we will try to distract him while it is going on.

My job is to talk to him, hold his head, keep his attention on me. Rikki will hold his hands and wrists wherever she can find places without casts, to keep him from thrashing while the nurses change the dressings on his leg. I confess that never in my life have I desired any kind of medical career. I hate looking at injuries, particularly other people's. I hate blood, scrapes, cuts, punctures, vomit, mucous blobs, ingrown toenails, mosquito bites, attached ticks, long abdominal gouges, rashes, bones sticking through skin, gum disease, you name it. As a result, I am committed to keeping my eyes on Arthur's face, so I won't have to look at whatever is brewing in his leg.

When the nurses are ready to start, I begin my patter. I talk about Wally and his broken leg and crutches, then move on to the Ronald McDonald House and our rooms and the aquarium, then talk about Dad and Marcia, John and Chris, Ann, Cherise, Rikki. Every so often, I make sure I have Arthur's attention. I hold his head, try to get him to look at me.

"Arthur, are you listening to my stories?"

"Hey, Hon, yes, I'm listening, but I'm in the middle of a meeting here. We're deciding whether to take a case."

"You can go back to the meeting soon, Arthur, right

now I want to talk to you."

"Oh, sure. Is somebody taking notes? Can we get that information? We have to talk to some of the sushi workers, make sure we have the story correct."

"What sushi workers?" I say.

"That's what this case is about. We have to talk to the sushi workers. Leslie, can you do that?"

Pretty sure I'm not going to get anything clearer on this. I hope this bandage change will be finished soon. If I have to move on to talking about Russian literature or Emily Dickinson, both subjects I love, I will lose Arthur's attention for sure.

I hear the nurses talk about having to be careful because of the infection. I look over at Rikki, who is standing to my right, and then glance down at the bed, expecting to see clean, new bandages. Instead, there is Arthur's lower leg. I don't know what I'm looking at. It is part of Arthur, and I can see bones but nothing else that looks like the inside of a body. Green liquid. I see green liquid the color of the skin of Granny Smith apples. No muscles, nothing but bones and green liquid.

My throat tightens; I fight against the gag reflex. I turn back to Arthur's face and make sounds, maybe word sounds, maybe not. I start talking about Jeff Foote and the 800 number, while my throat feels as if it weighs a hundred pounds and is pushing down on my chest at the same time that it is pushing half-digested food up and out. The 800 number, all the people who have been calling. I'm reaching for names just to say them — there's Marti Wivell, who called to tell Arthur to remember that there must be a pony in this huge pile of horseshit.

"Arthur, are you paying attention?" I say.

"Yes, I'm listening, but I have to get back to the meeting."

Even in his head-injured state, Arthur is trying to be helpful, accommodating. That's part of what has always made him so easy to be with. He's the happiest person I have ever known, not fake happy, not pretending — really happy. Throughout our marriage I have joked with him about it, telling him no one could be as happy as he is. And he responds with, "So how did I end up with a moody and difficult person?" Just lucky, I tell him.

*Get lucky now, Arthur. Get through this. Come back to me.*

"Okay, we're done," the nurse announces. I have lost track of how time moves. It feels as if I've been standing here talking for three hours. I don't know the actual time.

I kiss Arthur and say, "You can go back to your meeting now," but he's already gone into another present tense.

Rikki and I look at each other.

"Can I talk to you in the hall?" I ask.

"Yeah," she says. "I have to say, I have never heard you talk that much or that fast about anything. I was amazed."

"Me too. I felt as if I just had to keep the motor going."

Outside the room, I tell her I can't determine what's real anymore.

"Was the inside of his leg green? It looked to me like it was green. Where it was supposed to be muscles and red blood, was it green?"

"Yes," she says.

"Green, like apples? That kind of green? His leg?"
"Yes. It was green."
*Why is she not surprised by that?*

Al, Marcia, Rikki, and I are sitting in a lounge waiting for the two orthopedic surgeons who are operating on Arthur. Wrist and leg on the docket today. In addition to learning about Arthur's condition, I want to talk to these two about how soon I can move Arthur and where I should be looking to place him. I'm caught between taking care of Arthur and taking care of Wally. We've been here for ten days. Wally needs to get back to school; Arthur needs to stay in the hospital. I need some direction about how to manage this.

The table lamps are on even though it's only six or seven o'clock in the evening. The lounge reminds me of the early American living room décor I saw in my aunts' houses when I was growing up: maple furniture, dark patterned fabric on the sofas, end tables with lamps, magazines on a coffee table. I half expect the stuffy smell that accompanied most shotgun houses, old cooking odors having migrated from the kitchen and taken up residence in the stuffed furniture.

The doctors walk in, looking tired, sounding tired.

"Arthur made it through both surgeries. We repaired his wrist as much as we can now and tried to clear out the infection in his leg. Now we have to see how he does in recovery."

Leg doc is speaking.

"I just need to ask this," I say. "Is Arthur still in danger of dying?"

"Given the extent of his injuries, that remains a possibility. Every day he makes it through is good."

"I also need to ask you about the possibility of moving him. My son needs to get back to school, and I have to start making arrangements for Arthur to move to a hospital nearer our home in Oakland."

The docs look at each other.

Wrist doc says, "We can't advise moving him now. We'd like to keep him here at least for a couple more weeks, if not months. He has extensive injuries that will take numerous surgeries to repair."

We are all silent.

Finally I say, "I would love to stay here. It would make everything so much easier and I know Arthur is getting great care, but I have a seven-year-old who has been severely traumatized and I need to get him back to some kind of normal life as soon as possible. He needs to be among his friends, people he knows, his dog, a familiar space. I can't give Wally a normal life without moving Arthur. Is there any way we can do that?"

Leg doc says, "We can't allow you to move him anywhere but a trauma hospital. He needs surgeons trained to deal with the complex injuries he has. But again, we advise against moving him anytime soon."

"If I could find a hospital and orthopedic surgeons who are trauma-trained, would you take a look at their qualifications, let us know what you think?"

"That's the only way we'd feel comfortable releasing him."

Wally wakes me up this morning and says, "Want to hear my dream?"

"Sure."

"I was in a room with a scare-device thing and it would keep popping in and out."

"You mean like a jack-in-the-box?" I ask.

"Yes, like that. And when anybody would scream at it, it would scream too. I think the scare-device was more like a pop-up snake. There was too much screaming. I had to wake up."

I hold onto him to help us both feel better. I am so tired, emotionally and physically exhausted. I'm tired when I wake up, in Arthur's room, eating, talking on the phone, going to bed, all the time tired.

I spend a long time in the shower this morning. I can finally scrub my head. I try to get off the scabs and crusted blood left over from all the staples and stitches. There are patches of shaved hair and stitches all over. Washing it feels good.

When I get dressed and go to the medical center, I start again trying to arrange to move Arthur back home. There are only three hospitals with trauma surgeons in the Bay Area: one in San Francisco, one in Walnut Creek, and one in Oakland. I have to take into account physicians, convenience, safety, physical therapy departments, even ease of parking. We have no idea how long Arthur will need to be hospitalized, so wherever he goes has to meet a lot of requirements.

This process requires phone calls, decisions, forms. I talk to doctors, lawyers, social workers, case managers. I call everyone I can think of who has connections to any of these hospitals. Before I can move Arthur, I have to have agreements from a hospital with a bed for him; an orthopedic traumatologist willing to take him on as a patient; AirLife, which will transport us to the California hospital; and I have to get an insurance company to pay for the transit. This is why hospitals have social workers and case managers: one hurting person could never coordinate all these elements.

I get a call from Kris Cross, Wally's respiratory therapist at his CF clinic back home. I know her well because she, Ann, Cherise, Cherise's boyfriend, Geoff, and I all trained for and ran the Kona Marathon this past June to raise money for the Cystic Fibrosis Foundation. I contacted Kris because she also works at John Muir Medical Center, the trauma hospital in Walnut Creek; I asked if she could track down the best orthopedic surgeon there. Kris tells me she has talked to many people, and the person I want is Chris Coufal, who specializes in legs. She says everyone she has spoken to told her that he's the guy who does what no one else can.

If I can get Dr. Coufal to take Arthur on, this might work out. I have pretty much decided John Muir is where we ought to go. Even though it is farther from home than the hospital in Oakland, it has more parking and easier access for late-night visits and calls at any time. Wally's pulmonologist also has an office near John Muir, so I could get him in easily if he had any CF complications. Now all I have to do is get this all coordinated.

My goal right now is to move Arthur early next week. Wally has already missed two weeks of school — if he can be back with his friends, at a school he knows, at least something will seem familiar. I've already called the school's director, a child-life specialist, and asked her if she can find a child psychologist for him who specializes in trauma.

Whatever happens with Arthur's transport, Cherise has agreed to drive Wally back to Oakland on Monday. He can stay with Geoff and her until I get back to the Bay Area. Wally says he's comfortable with this arrangement; he wants to go home. Of course, I worry about his being in a car for ten hours driving there. I worry about him being anywhere I can't see him — and even where I can.

I'll have to spend tomorrow packing up Wally's and Arthur's and some of my belongings so Cherise can take them back in the car with her. I will be going on the plane with Arthur, so I'll only be able to take a small suitcase. I still don't know what we have; it can't be that much. Wally and I keep re-wearing the same clothes that Marcia washes for us.

I just put Wally in the car with Cherise and said good-bye to them. It feels so dangerous to let them go out into the world. Wally, however, is in fine spirits, giving me hugs because I am crying and trying not to cry when I say good-bye. He's eager to get out in the sunny, warm day, wanting to go home, be away from hospitals. Me too. Cherise is a genius. She has given Wally jobs for the road. Last night she taught him how to use her cell phone. Today he is supposed to call me every hour to let me know where they are and how they are doing. She also told him he has to check out the restaurants to stop at along the way and to decide where and when they should take breaks.

I go back to Dr. Friesse this morning, so he can remove the stitches below my left eye. While I'm there he also extracts a quarter-inch-square piece of glass from my right eyelid. He tells me to go to an ophthalmologist in a couple, three weeks, just to make sure there are no complications with my eye as the result of the blowout fracture.

About four o'clock this afternoon, all the pieces fall together. We can leave with Arthur tomorrow at noon. He's got a bed, a doctor, and a medical transport plane waiting for him. As I gather up everything, I have jumbled feelings. This hospital has been excellent and safe, all the people wonderful. I know I want to go home, but, if Wally didn't have to get back to school, I think Arthur and

I would stay here. It would be so much easier than making this move with Arthur still so fragile.

I tell him that we're leaving tomorrow, but he is in whatever place his brain inhabits right now. I am alone at his bedside.

Thank goodness for my father-in-law. I am a nervous flier
and have a prescription for Xanax, just for flying; however, I don't have any with me. Last night when Al asked
me if there was anything he could do to help, I told him:
Get me some Xanax. An hour on a tiny medical transport plane with a babbling husband could send me right
out the plane door into the stratosphere. This morning
Al hands me a small vial with three pills in it, and I don't
care if he broke into the pharmacy and stole them, I am
grateful.

Wally and Cherise called me when they reached
Oakland last night. They had a long, but uneventful trip,
which involved numerous phone calls and many stops
at Taco Bells along the way. Rikki left Bend on Saturday,
and Al and Marcia will fly out early tomorrow morning.
They want to stay here until they are sure we made it to
John Muir without complications. I am supposed to show
up at the AirLife office at noon. AirLife is in this medical
complex too. It seems as if everything is within walking
distance — the docs, the transport, the psychologists. St.
Charles makes it easy to have a trauma.

By the time I get checked in and to the hangar, Arthur
is already on board the plane. I meet the pilot, co-pilot,
and EMT who are on this ride. Including Arthur and me,
that makes five of us. I sit in the back, behind Arthur's
stretcher, with my suitcase at my feet. The EMT sits next

to Arthur, who is neither conscious nor unconscious at this moment. Another one of those clear Oregon days. I take a pill.

Okay, this is going all right. The EMT is talking to me about why she likes her job; everyone is relaxed, friendly. I'm looking out the window even though I don't like doing that on airplanes. We're flying low. How far can it be to the ground? I figure we should be in Concord, California, where we're landing, in about forty-five more minutes. Then we'll get Arthur into an ambulance and drive another forty-five minutes to the medical center.

The EMT has just gone up to talk to the pilot. I can tell by the way they are talking that something's not right. She comes back and tells me there's a problem with the altimeter, and the pilot will feel better returning to Bend and switching planes.

*Oh, come on.*

This won't be a big problem, she tells me. There is another plane available that we can take instead; this will only hold us up for an hour or so. I dig in my bag for another Xanax. I don't know if the story about the altimeter is true. I don't even know what an altimeter is. The crew members all seem cool, but that's how they're trained to appear.

*Shit, shit, shit.*

The ride back gets really bumpy. What does an altimeter have to do with the bump factor? I wonder what's really wrong with this plane.

*Just get us down. Be calm. Look, Arthur's not worried about anything. But Arthur doesn't even know he's in a plane. He's probably off swimming in the Hawaiian surf.*

We land smoothly. I think the panic must have been only mine since everyone else is still cool and collected. They tell me it will be half an hour or so until we take off again. I don't have a book with me. All my books were lost except *Kavalier & Clay,* and I sent that home with Cherise. That was another thing John found. He held it up to show me — blood spatters on the pages. When he handed the book to me and I turned it over, glass and dirt fell out of the pages.

I sit in the waiting room, look at magazines, and write in my journal until it's time to head out again. One of my spiral-bound notebooks survived, and I've been writing in it several times a day. I decided pretty soon after I was conscious that I wanted to keep track of everything that was happening to us. They have already moved Arthur to the new plane, and we're set to go. I take the last Xanax and hope I will be coherent when we get to Concord. After Arthur gets settled in at the new hospital, I will call Cherise and she'll come pick me up and take me home. That could be much later. But right now, I intend to sleep through this flight.

## GREEN APPLE QUICK STEP, IF YOU'VE GOT
## THE LEGS FOR IT

Maybe it's all about expectations, but don't you wonder why Rikki didn't think green goop inside a leg was unusual? If you saw someone's leg opened up and the inside was green, and this person wasn't a Martian or high on copper, wouldn't you think it peculiar? So what was with Rikki that she didn't?

Maybe when you're expecting death, everything else is tolerable. While Rikki knew and understood that Arthur could die at any time, Dervs didn't know that. Her mind wasn't able to bend that way. Our minds protect us, and Dervs's mind was keeping the possibility of Arthur's death out of her line of sight. She was watching robins and sparrows flick their wings in a cast-stone bird bath outside the window, watching the sun paint the water's surface, turn it iridescent and sparkling. What was supposed to be green: grass, luna moths, jealousy, bamboo, the lime in a gin and tonic.

Even seeing the green leg didn't set off certain warning bells for Dervs. For instance, she didn't think about the possibility of amputation if the infection got too bad. Yet Dervs was obsessed with World War One. She was held captive by that war, and she surely knew about amputation after amputation that took place. She knew too about the surgeries to reconstruct soldiers' faces, the plastic surgeries that failed and melted or slipped away, leaving patients further disfigured or dead. She knew that a man who went off to that war never came home; what came home was a different version of a man, sometimes unrecognizable, even to his family, even when his face remained intact.

Arthur's injuries were not unlike those of soldiers coming back from war. The weapon was different, but so many parts were broken. He was going to have to face life with a body unlike any he could have imagined.

Choosing a hospital is like choosing a spouse: You hope for one solid constant, in this case, excellent care. The rest of it is up for grabs. I have a friend who has had a medical career for years and who says that medicine doesn't move on the same schedule as everything else, that it is not a service industry, and that no one wants to admit it — and no one wants to believe it.

After I found a great surgeon, it turns out that he was out of town when we arrived at the hospital in California. Not his fault, the timing was bad. I was caught between sending Wally home without me or moving Arthur to a local, California hospital sooner than would have been optimal. No one knows how long Arthur will be hospitalized. It could be months, years, or for the rest of his life, and I will have to be running between places for that time. I think both Wally and I need a familiar place. It is so difficult to be sure of anything.

For now, I am doing my best to make sure Arthur has what *he* needs. In addition to a room and the right doctors, he needs someone to stay with him all the time. The head injury has caused him to become agitated quickly, and because he has so many injuries and casts, he needs to remain relatively immobile. Flailing around could cause serious orthopedic problems.

Somewhere along the line, I was given a sheet of paper with guidelines to help keep Arthur calm. The instructions, however, contain so many uppercase letters that I feel as if they are shouting at me.

*Ways to Decrease Agitation*
*— Reduce Noise*
*— Talk in a Calm, Soothing Voice*
*— Give Simple Directions*
*— Speak Slowly*
*— Avoid Too Many Visitors or Staff in the room*
  *at one time*
*— Review Orientation Frequently throughout*
  *the day*
*— Approach the Patient Slowly and Quietly*
*— Try to keep a Daily Routine*
       *Thank you!*

The English professor in me is throwing up. Can I trust people who use this kind of punctuation — all those capital letters yelling at me to be quiet? Trust them or not, Arthur's got to be kept calm, so we have to hire someone — a monitor is the job title — to sit with him when no family member or friend is present. Apparently television is one of the things that can overload a head injury; the monitor needs to keep the TV off and keep the noise level down.

I worry sometimes about my own head injury. I see my GP tomorrow; maybe she can give me some help on this. The docs at St. Charles advised me to have a battery of tests to determine how my thinking may have been affected by the injury. How could I know at this point? I can say that the one thing I crave is quiet. I want to sleep for a long time and wake up to find someone else has dealt with everything and Arthur is home and fine and we're just going to go on with our lives. Otherwise, I will find that I have lost my best friend, and I don't know what to do about it.

Word gets around fast. Neighbors and friends are showing up with food, offers to take Wally out while I go to the hospital. The days are filled with medical appointments, meetings, hospital visits. If I had had a nine-to-five job before the accident, I would have had to quit. As it is, I have no time to work, no time to write except for in the journal I carry around. Whatever this is I am doing, it is more than full time, taking more time than I have. Poor Vinnie, our dog. I picked him up from the boarder's house last Wednesday and he hasn't seen much of us since, although Wally spends a lot of time hugging him. Vinnie is a huge, white and black borzoi with the silkiest fur imaginable, a magnificent place to get lost, especially if you are seven.

Today Wally and I are sitting in a waiting room at the orthopedic center of Children's Hospital in Oakland. We are here to have Wally's cast changed. The room is getting more and more crowded. Wally is playing Nintendo with another child who is waiting for treatment. A TV is tuned to *Blue's Clues*. The adults in the room are taking up a lot of space. One woman is talking to herself about big boogers. Another is complaining about how she has eleven kids and doesn't want any of them. I wish my blue, molded plastic chair were a spaceship and I could zoom out of here in it.

Earlier this morning, before I picked Wally up from

school to bring him here, I met with the school's director to discuss what Wally, and I, might need. She says Wally's trauma could take many forms and that she has alerted the teachers and student teachers not to push him. She also recommended a child psychologist who specializes in childhood trauma.

When we finally get in to see the children's doctor assigned to Wally, he asks me if I hurt my face in the same accident in which Wally hurt his leg. This is not a good appointment. Wally is traumatized by the machine that cuts the cast off his leg and screams during the entire procedure. The technicians are doing all the right things; it doesn't matter. Wally has to scream. We all want to scream, but he's the only one who seems comfortable doing it. He will now have a walking cast for three weeks. That should be easier to deal with.

When we are finished here, I'll take Wally back to school and then go over to John Muir hospital. Rikki is with Arthur now, so I know he is attended to. We hope to get some specific notion of timing this week. My understanding is that Arthur is scheduled for two operations — one on his ankle and one on his hand. I think the one on his ankle is slated for Wednesday. I hope that's right. I have my first appointment with a psychologist tomorrow.

I have the directions and the code to unlock the door. The steps leading up to her office are clean, and I manage to get into a small waiting area with two chairs separated by a table piled with art books and current *New Yorker* magazines. I flip the switch on the wall inside the door to let her know I've arrived. I am wary of therapists, being of the too-much-introspection-may-not-be-a-good-thing school.

A door opens and a petite blonde woman says, "Nancy? I am Charlotte. Come on in."

We walk through another door and into an L-shaped office with pale yellow walls. She points me to a leather chair in the longer leg of the L; she sits in another close by. I am not really listening to what she is saying. I want to check her out, see how I feel about her. I don't want to be spilling my guts to somebody I don't feel good about. Here's what I like: She has edges; I can see where she begins and ends. She is not taking up too much space in the room. She is wearing a black skirt, dark tights, and low heels with a brown jacket that has some style to it; a therapist wearing a big flowery outfit would send me straight out the door. She has a nice voice, well modulated, no screeches, and she seems sympathetic, although I suppose that's her job.

In addition to psychology books, there are volumes of poetry in a glass-fronted bookcase — Wallace Stevens,

Emily Dickinson, Elizabeth Bishop, Anne Michaels. I think there might be hope. Even though I haven't published a book of poems since 1996, I write all the time. I am, however, a perpetually lazy office manager and don't send my work out as I should. That was going to be one of my projects for this fall — getting my work out — that and trying to write something about cystic fibrosis and the impact of living in a medical miasma.

Now Charlotte is asking me to tell her what happened. I make it through five steely sentences and start to cry.

When I was six, I had my tonsils taken out because I had frequent earaches. I was in a ward with maybe ten beds filled with children, all of whom were having their tonsils removed. When my parents dropped me off in the morning, the nurse told them they could pick me up any time after ten o'clock the next morning. That night, after the operation, I was afraid and crying so much that the nurse told me if I didn't stop making noise I wouldn't be allowed to have ice cream with the other kids. I don't remember if I stopped or not, just that the next morning I was so eager for my parents to pick me up that I kept my eyes on the clock starting at seven. At ten o'clock I breathed a sigh. I would be out soon. Sets of smiling parents began arriving and each time I looked for familiar faces. Then it was ten thirty and all the kids except me and one other had left. That child's parents came, and I was left in the ward alone until eleven thirty, when my parents finally appeared. When I asked why they were so late, they told me they had some chores to do first. I don't know why I think of this as I tell Charlotte about the crash.

At the end of the session, she asks me if I want to continue with her, and I tell her yes. We set up times to meet each Tuesday and Thursday.

I'm in the aquarium room at John Muir, watching what I think is an angelfish and waiting for Arthur to come out of surgery. Chris Coufal is rebuilding Arthur's right ankle. The surgery was supposed to start at 12:30 p.m., but Arthur didn't go to the operating room until 1:45, which turned out to be just fine since I didn't get here until 12:45. The whole day has been off-kilter.

At 6:45 this morning, the burglar alarm in our house went off and so did the backyard sprinkler system. I took Wally to school and when I returned home about nine, the sprinklers were still going. I called the guy who installed the system a couple years ago, and he was nice enough to repair it right away.

I headed out to meet our workers' compensation lawyer, Frank Russo, at ten. I spent an hour there, trying to get all the application forms filled out. Since Arthur was returning from working at the Sunriver conference, the accident should be covered under workers' comp. That's the reality. However, the insurance company is fighting the claim, saying that Arthur wasn't working. I have friends who are lawyers, who can advise me on all these machinations. How do people who don't have the same access deal with all this? You do everything right, and you still get screwed.

After meeting with Frank, I went home to gather books and my journal — things to occupy me while

Arthur was in surgery. When I got to the car, the damned thing wouldn't start, so I called Cherise to see if she could drive me to the hospital. She asked me if I would be more comfortable in her car or Geoff's and said she could even rent one if I wanted. I had no idea what she was even asking me.

"Do you want me to decide?" she said.

*Yes.*

I will have to deal with the car after I get home tonight. Right now, Wally is staying with friends. However, he has an appointment with his pediatric pulmonologist, the CF doc, tomorrow, so I've got to have some transportation to get him there.

I'm frazzled and frustrated about almost everything these days, so why not the car too? Add that to trying to get all the right people in to see Arthur. In a hospital this large, coordinating between departments is difficult, if not impossible. It feels as if I have to meet someone new every day. Yesterday it was the occupational therapist, who is different from the physical therapist. My friend Amy drove me to the hospital yesterday about eleven. Amy says I'm too tired to keep doing all this driving, that when she's around, she will drive me. When we got to Arthur's room, Rikki was already there. I think she comes over here right after she drops her kids at school, so she arrives before I do most days. She said she wanted to be here early to meet with the occupational therapist, so she could talk to him about Arthur's condition.

I walked in and felt as if I had entered a different universe. Rikki was making some kind of arrangements with a nurse, she had opened Arthur's mail, filled out his menus. She kept calling him "Love Boy" and "Sweet Pip." For a second, I thought, *Wait, am I his sister and not his wife? What's going on?* And I felt as if she was making faces at me for coming with Amy to the hospital.

Arthur was telling Amy to take notes on the imaginary sushi workers' case, Rikki had brought a cinnamon roll and was feeding it to Arthur, hospital personnel walked in and out, took tests, cleaned the room. I was trying to hold onto something, to place my mind somewhere, but there was too much movement. I could understand how Arthur could be over-stimulated; I was. Too much stimulation — what the head-injured among us are supposed to avoid.

On the drive home, Amy said she thought Rikki needed to do those things for herself, so she could feel better. I was reminded of someone at the hospital in Bend who said to me that Arthur's family was "well-intentioned, but they sure were needy." I have no idea how I fit into this frame. We are all messed up. When disaster hits, the best you can hope for is to get through it with some level of competency. Under this kind of stress, bizarre behavior becomes the commonplace. Some days I'm surprised that we're not all raving.

The worst part of this is that the person I want to talk to about it is Arthur. It's been three weeks, but it feels like three years. I have to work to remember our lives before this crash — the three of us hanging out in the front yard with Vinnie, Arthur and Wally playing basketball in the driveway, going to Wally's favorite sushi-boat restaurant.

What happens now is that Arthur and I have a nice, quiet moment and I have some hope for his recovery and then it shatters. Yesterday Rikki and I were sitting quietly with Arthur in his room, and he said to me, "Nancy, can you get these pants for me? Get the pants." Part of him is still back there in the car. A little later I asked him a choice question: "Do you want the apple juice or the sandwich?" Rikki looked at me and said, "You shouldn't ask him questions where he has to make a choice." I wanted to knock her head off. And then I wanted to talk to Arthur about it. Instead I draw further into myself, too tired to do anything.

Now, nervous trumps tired. It's six o'clock and there's no news about the surgery. I remember a waiting room like this at Children's Hospital in Washington, D.C. Wally was five months old and having a hernia operation. It was supposed to take forty-five minutes and instead took two hours. I was a wreck. Arthur kept telling me everything was going to be all right, and it was. That is Arthur's job in my life. He's the optimistic one, who says we can get through anything, and I believe him. It's part of who we are as a pair. He says, "Have I ever lied to you about this?" I say, "No." And now some asshole has fucked him up so much he might never reassure me again.

Cherise and Geoff walk in, tall and beautiful, Cherise with her mixed-race skin and curly hair, Geoff a blue-eyed blond. They have come to stay with me and take me home when Arthur's out of surgery.

"This is too hard," I say to Cherise.

At 8:15 p.m., Dr. Coufal comes into the room and tells

us that everything went well. It took a long time because the ankle was pretty much a jumble. Arthur will sleep through the night. We will go pick up Wally and get him home to bed. I'll get up early to deal with the car. I can't do anything more now.

I have slept twelve hours. I get up, still groggy, and try to turn off the house alarm. Instead, I set it off. The high-pitched, incessant wail shoots through me and seems to root me to the floor. Wally, in his bed, starts screaming. I can't figure out how to turn off the screeching. I hit every combination of buttons I can imagine but can't shut it off. Wally screams louder. By the time I hit the right sequence and shut down the alarm, my son is standing next to me in hysterics. He is holding his ears, his body is shaking, his mouth is misshapen and howling. My ears hurt too. I feel incapable of getting anything right.

We drive through the Caldecott Tunnel and to John Muir Medical Center about one o'clock. Wally sits in a corner chair in Arthur's room playing a hand-held video game while I talk with Arthur, who knows something is wrong, but he doesn't know what.

"Here's the problem," says Arthur. "I say something that seems simple and makes sense, and they all agree. But then they all start arguing. It's so frustrating. I can't keep them from arguing."

*Who is he talking about — all the voices in his head, all the different people who are parts of him, or who he was at different times in his life?*

He starts to cry. And then he cries more when he looks over at Wally and he talks about "that angel-faced boy." This is the man who, before the crash, made sense and jokes, who once finished a *New York Times* Sunday crossword in fifteen minutes, and when I looked at it had filled the spaces with gibberish because he knew I would find that hilarious.

Just before we get ready to leave, a doctor comes by and introduces himself as a hospitalist.

*What the hell is a hospitalist? How did I miss the evolution of all this hospital jargon?*

I suppose a hospitalist is a person who evaluates head injuries. I don't know, and he doesn't tell me. What he does is ask Arthur a couple questions:

Q: Do you know where you live?

A: No. I can't be sure.

Q: What year is it?

A: Virginia.

I want to grab the man lying in the bed by the shoulders, make him look at me, and say, "Just answer the damn question! You know what year it is!"

I don't. He doesn't.

I feel as if I could grab Wally's hand, walk out the door, and keep going. We could find a place in Arizona, where I would invent a new story for us. I'd get a job working as an organization expert, make lots of money, say I was a single mom, and no one would notice us for a while, until we had spent several years in our new personas. We'd have to choose new names: Ariel and Victor maybe. After five years, Wally would be in middle school, we'd be comfortable enough to be in the world more. Wally would play guitar in a fledgling rock band; I'd start going to movies with smart and witty men.

In today's reality, Charlotte has told me that I am angry into the ineffable with Arthur because he spent years assuring me he would always be there and I could rely on him for anything — and it turns out he wasn't telling the truth.

## TELL THEM TO SPEAK SLOWLY. I'M FINE.

Let's just come out and say it: People in this story are going to communicate in eccentric ways. Maybe the ways are not so much outside the norm, it's just that some of the characters are willing to admit to them. For example, Ann called Dervs one morning and told her Arthur's brain was coming back.

"Listen," she said, "Arthur is going to be all right. It will just take a little more time. I had a dream last night, and in this dream, Arthur was talking to me from the hospital bed. He said, 'Tell them to speak slowly. I'm fine.' So I'm telling you: when you talk to him, speak slowly. It's taking him longer to process everything now, but he's going to be all right. He's coming back. I'm telling you this is true."

Dervs believed her, and she was right to believe her because after six weeks of drifting and weaving in his head, Arthur woke up one morning. Here's how it happened.

Arthur opened his eyes and saw an unfamiliar, white-coated figure, a man, sitting by the right side of his bed. The man's face wasn't clear, and Arthur was having a hard time focusing. Everything felt hazy.

"Mr. Bryant?" said the man.

Arthur couldn't figure out, was this a dream? Or was it happening in real time? The man had a strong voice. Arthur liked that, thought he might talk to this man.

"Yes," Arthur said.

"Mr. Bryant, I'm a doctor, and I'm sorry to bother you, but can you tell me what day it is, what month it is, and what city we're in?"

Arthur wasn't certain about the answers to any of these questions. It was hard to get his mouth to form words.

"I'm not sure, but I think, I'm guessing now, that it's August, we're in Oregon, and I don't know what day it is."

"Those are all good guesses, Mr. Bryant, but they are all wrong."

"I'm sorry. I'm just waking up. I took a nap."

"No, you didn't."

"Yes, I did," said Arthur.

"No, Mr. Bryant. Let me tell you what happened while you thought you took a nap. You were in a horrible car crash. Everyone thought you were going to die. You had numerous injuries. Your lungs collapsed and you had multiple broken bones in all of your limbs. Your wife was also seriously injured, but she's okay now. Your son had a broken leg, and he's all right now too. For six weeks, you've had somebody sitting by your bed to see if your brain would return."

"Get the hell out of here! I was taking a nap."

"No. Mr. Bryant, if you look down, you'll see your body in bandages."

Arthur could make out long tunnels of blue where his legs and arms should be. His sight wasn't clear, but this man's voice sounded authoritative, calm. Maybe he was telling the truth.

Other people were coming and going, he knew this. They were talking to him about the accident. He must have gone back to sleep because that same doctor wasn't there. Everything was so fuzzy. He started to think of the doctor as the *straight man* because it felt as though he was telling it straight, directly. Arthur was trying to work this all out in his head.

And then he was back, the doctor, saying, "I know this may be hard for you to believe, but you need to understand that you are incredibly lucky."

"Lucky?" said Arthur. "Were you paying attention? I thought I took a nap, and you told me my body and my world have been blown up. I'm not feeling lucky."

"I understand how you feel," the straight man said, "but almost no one would have survived that crash. The few that did, their brains would never have returned. If your brain is back, your body will heal. And that makes you incredibly lucky."

The longer they spoke, the more Arthur began to believe this man whom he couldn't fully see, but whose voice was reassuring, like the voice of his father when Arthur was a child. The man's voice was calm; he must be right.

When Dervs came in the next morning, Arthur was sitting up in bed, smiling.

He said, "Hi, Honey. I'm back."

She looked at him.

"I'm back. I woke up."

She didn't start to cry, she didn't run to his side

and embrace him, cover him with kisses, tell him how much she missed him. She stood in the greenish light of his hospital room looking at him, at his six-week growth of beard, thinking he should get a shave.

"It's true," Arthur said. "I know what happened. The doctor will confirm it. I woke up, and I know where I am and what's going on. I'm not saying I believe it all; it's going to take a while to sink in. But the important thing is that I'm back."

He was making sense. He wasn't talking about living in D.C. in 1990 or about farts or about Muhammad Ali. He wasn't speaking in non sequiturs or laughing at jokes where the punch line was in his head. He wasn't telling Amy to take dictation about the case involving the sushi workers, but he was still speaking in that voice, what Dervs thought of as the *head injury voice*. It was a tone higher than his normal speaking voice, and phlegmy — as if he had a perpetual blob of mucous stuck in his throat. And it was flat, without much affect.

Could she believe he was back if he announced it in the *head injury voice*?

Everyone told her it was a miracle. They said it would take time for him to recover fully, if he ever did; however, Arthur was present for the first time in six weeks. He had come back.

But that voice dug into her. It would hang on for several months and then continue to appear out of nowhere — in the middle of dinner, during a game of hearts, discussing a movie. Every time she heard it, she felt as if she was choking on the phlegm of it, swallowing a cup of egg whites, viscous and creepy in her throat, traveling down her body to rest in a cold and creepy wad in her stomach, which stayed until the voice went away and Arthur was speaking normally again.

For two years the voice did this, sometimes taking away her own voice. And then it disappeared. One day Dervs woke up and knew the voice was gone. Then it was safe to talk to Arthur about it, about the *head injury voice*. He asked her please to never call it that.

But back at the resurrection: there was much rejoicing — at the hospital and all through the land. Arthur himself called Rikki and his father, who called the rest of the family. Arthur called his assistant at his law firm; he called Jeff Foote; he called his friend Curtis. Everyone said the same thing — a miracle! Except the orthopedic surgeons, who said, "Now he's going to know how much pain he's in."

And Dervs, who wondered what you have to do to follow up a miracle. After certain miracles, people have disappeared.

One morning Dervs got up, took Wally to school, and then called Ann.

"I need to get a car. Today. Can you come with me?"

"Sure. When?"

"As soon as you can."

"Where are you going?

"The Volvo dealer. I want the safest car I can buy. I've checked, and I've got about seven thousand dollars. That's a pretty good down payment, isn't it?

"I think so. You know, most of my cars have been used when I bought them."

"Me too, but right now I need a car that's built like a tank with every possible safety feature. Then I'll figure out how to pay for it."

A Volvo station wagon says suburbs, prep schools, life in a fortress. Dervs had never imagined herself in such a car, not until the moment when she chose red over green. It was the end-of-the-year car sale. The showroom and lot were littered with choices.

"How about this green Cross Country?" Dervs said to Ann.

"Have you looked at the burgundy? I like that one." said Ann.

"Okay," Dervs told the salesman. "I'll take the red one."

An hour later, she drove it off the lot. At her

appointment the next morning, she told Charlotte about the car.

"Safe. It's safe. I have to protect against every possibility, be ready for anything, be ready for war."

Charlotte knew this. A couple weeks after they met, she had said that, even if Dervs had never mentioned her mother, she would have known that Dervs had had a psychotic parent. Children of whacked-out parents apparently have whole sets of behavior identifiers, peculiarities, residuals, moats and barriers, folding armor, stakes and knives they carry with them — in the event of attack.

The attacks had begun early. Dervs never could be quite sure when. The beatings with wooden spoons and belts weren't the real problem. They were tolerable. The real problem was the unexpected. Whatever couldn't be anticipated was what happened. Her mother swooped down out of trees, tall buildings, circus tents, anywhere there was enough room for the wings of a harpy. She plucked at Dervs's eyes and hair and skin, pinching, pinching. One night she came out onto the front porch, screaming, and pulled Dervs into the house by her hair while yelling at Dervs's boyfriend for bringing her home so late. Another time she started yelling at one of Dervs's friends for taking milk out of the refrigerator. There was no way to anticipate how she was going to behave.

At any given time she might have been chasing Dervs around the house, batting at her with three-inch spiked heels she had just taken off, aiming for the child's head. Dervs never knew what set off these attacks, but she became a planner — plans A, B, and C — for what to do in the event of battle.

Dervs's hope, all through her life, was to never open the box labeled "Mother." She wanted no therapy, no psychological excavation. She was functioning just fine without another invasion. But here she was with a therapist she needed, who was giving her psychological bandages, so she could go back into her ravaged world and deal with its demands. Here she was with this woman who wanted her to talk about her mother. No fucking way.

Instead Dervs told Charlotte the latest medical news. She showed up at Charlotte's office in tears some days, hysterical with anger on others. One morning she was driving to her appointment, drifting down the hill from her house, when she spotted a dead doe lying on the side of the road. People always drove too fast up and down this road. The doe had been recently hit; she hadn't been there ten minutes ago when Dervs had returned from taking Wally to school. The doe lay facing the road, her eyes wide open. Dervs stared at her and then realized another deer was standing next to the doe. A buck, antlers. They both seemed young. The buck was looking out into the road, and then he nudged the doe with his nose. When she didn't move, he looked back at the road.

The image drove right into the middle of Dervs's pain and she started screaming, crying in loud gulps, her face wet and distorted all the way to Charlotte's door. She told Charlotte what she had seen and that afterward she had put in a Leonard Cohen CD, and even that couldn't touch her sorrow. Dervs played Leonard Cohen all the time, especially when things were bleak. A friend gave her Cohen's first album when Dervs was living in Moscow, after college, and she had stacks of his CDs now. How could you not rely on a musician who loved García Lorca's poetry? Cohen's music had seen her through a series of life's disasters. She was saying this to Charlotte, glad to talk about García Lorca instead of roadkill, when Charlotte said, "So Leonard Cohen is your mother. His music gives you what your mother didn't — solace, comfort, company."

"Leonard Cohen is what my mother should have been. What my mother is? My mother is the accident: violent, unexpected, coming out of nowhere to chew up my life."

What you do following a miracle is make sure the resurrected is taken care of. At the end of September, Arthur's caseworker tells me that he can't be moved to the rehab section of John Muir because he is not weight bearing. Truth is, the only parts of his body that can bear any weight are his elbows. Our health insurer says it won't pay for Arthur to remain at John Muir because he doesn't need trauma care any longer. I suppose this is fair since he isn't allowed to do anything but lie in bed. It has been two months. No weight on his arms or legs, no moving, no walking, nothing to do but to sit up with help.

Arthur tells me again and again how difficult it is to be an invalid — "in valid," he says, as in, "if you can't move, you have no worth." Even before his cognition fully resurfaced, he said that. I need to get him out of here anyway. The head of neuropsychology has been telling us — Arthur's family members and even friends — what a difficult bunch we are to deal with. She says none of the staff likes us because we are too demanding. I don't think she likes having a group of patient advocates. My advice: Don't allow anyone you love into a hospital, no matter how good the facility, without someone watching over him or her. Too many patients, too few staff. Mistakes will be made. And there's a good chance no one will catch them but you.

The patient and family pay in every circumstance. I open the mail, medical bills from Oregon. Here's one for five thousand dollars. The insurance company attaches a check for two hundred dollars to cover it. This is where Jeff Foote comes in. I send him everything, and his office sorts it out.

"Don't cash any checks," he tells me. "You don't want them to think you are accepting two hundred dollars for a five-thousand-dollar bill."

I ask Ann how people manage this flood of bills, financial harassment on top of life-threatening trauma.

"They don't," she says. "They lose their houses; they lose everything. You guys are the lucky ones. You have people helping you."

She's right. When I didn't have a notion where the money to cover immediate medical expenses would come from, some friends of Arthur's got together and gave us fifty thousand dollars. They just gave it to us — all that money — because they love Arthur and because they know when trauma strikes, you need love and you need money. And the money flies out to pay medical bills. No matter how good the health insurance is, trauma costs more than you could imagine, and there is no way most of us can ever prepare for it.

To get him out of John Muir, Arthur's caseworker recommends that he move to Kentfield Rehabilitation Hospital in Marin County — north and west across the San Francisco Bay from where we live — about an hour away if there are no traffic problems. The caseworker shepherds us through the application process, which includes waiting a week for approval from the insurance company (the same one that says it won't pay for him to stay where he is). Arthur is cleared to move on October 8 and finally does move on the seventeenth.

I am packing up his room — 478 West Wing — after nearly six weeks. I'm putting away eight-by-ten family photographs; books that friends have sent, although Arthur still can't read because he has double vision; magazines; stuffed animals — a pony, two bears; plants; and foot-high singing characters in the form of Ray Charles and a turtle. I didn't know turtles were singers. There are boxes of get-well cards, hundreds of them. We've been reading the cards to Arthur from the beginning, but now I am packing them away, so he can take time to look at them when he finally gets home.

Kentfield is a hospital that treats patients who have had serious physical injuries in addition to a traumatic head injury. The woman who heads the facility, Debra Doherty, is a physiatrist, a physician who specializes in physical medicine and rehabilitation — I add *physiatrist* to *hospitalist* on my list of new medical specialties.

Arthur's move goes smoothly, and we all relax a little as he settles in. This hospital is small, only one floor, and we hope the staff members get to know the patients well. This is where Arthur will have physical therapy, where he will learn to walk again, where he will begin to use his right hand to write again. From his bed, situated in the center of the room against a wall, he can see outside through a large window on his right. On the wall opposite the window is a sofa. There is a bedside table and a couple chairs, a bathroom, a cupboard. This room will be his residence for months; we don't know how long.

A couple of days before Halloween, Wally sits on the sofa. Arthur asks him about his costume.

"I don't think I'm going to dress up this year," says Wally.

"Why not?" says Arthur.

"I think that in the past I've made a fool of myself, particularly as Tigger, and I don't want to do that again."

"Everybody looks kind of silly on Halloween. That's part of the fun, isn't it?" says Arthur.

"I don't know. If I could take my bike to school, I'd go as a BMXer."

Wally's choice to replace his bicycle that was destroyed in the crash was a red BMX bike, complete with foot pegs.

"You could go like a pirate, and we could be twins," says Arthur, referring to the eye patch he's been wearing over his left eye to combat the double vision. The diagnosis so far is that two different muscles are competing for dominance in his eye. He had a CT scan yesterday in attempts to figure out exactly what's happening.

"No, Dad, I don't want to be a pirate."

I think that Arthur's face falls in a little, but it's hard to tell. His head has become a lot furrier in the last two months. He hasn't had a shave or haircut, and his dark brown curly hair is moving in all directions. I've never seen him with a beard before; he does look like a pirate. Another benefit of Kentfield is that a barber comes in on a regular schedule. I hope he comes soon.

Wally doesn't dress up for school, but he does go out with friends on Halloween night. He patches together a costume as an evil spirit. We find a mask and cape and staff of some sort. This is a pro forma exercise for us both; we do it because it is Halloween, and we should. Our hearts aren't in it, but Wally has a good time, and for once, I don't care if he eats all the candy in the world.

On weekends I've been taking him to the local park, so he can ride his bicycle. I outfit him with helmet and elbow and kneepads, and I sit on a bench and pretend to read while he makes up tricks. He begins by standing on the back pegs of the bike while holding onto the handlebars. Then he gets braver and stands on one peg with his other leg up in the air. The kid has good balance.

In a couple weeks he gets the bike going and then stands on the seat, bending over to hold onto the handlebars. The culmination of this trick is that he sticks one leg up in the air and lets go of one of the handlebars. It's all I can do not to run over and drag him off the thing. But I sit on my bench and tell him what a great job he's doing. I've talked to his therapist about this, and he tells me that this is Wally's way of gaining some control after his world has gone haywire. He's trying to gain control over a vehicle. This makes sense to me, and I hope Wally can keep from flying off and breaking his neck.

I had told Wally that when the cast came off his leg, I'd buy him a new bicycle. When the technician cut off his cast, Wally screamed uncontrollably — it was as if the man was sawing off his leg. I think Wally just needed to yell at the unfairness of the whole situation. For a week after the cast was taken off, he walked with a limp, as if he couldn't jostle the echo of injustice out of his leg. I wouldn't have foreseen that a couple weeks later he would be flying around like this.

## AURA BOREALIS

A couple of days before Thanksgiving Dervs was waiting for a haircut, reading *People* magazine in the lounge area, when a woman walked in and looked at her sitting there. The woman studied Dervs for a couple minutes, which Dervs didn't notice because, after all, it was *People* magazine. The woman walked across the room and stood in front of Dervs.

"You look like an angel," she said.

"What?" said Dervs.

"You look like an angel."

Dervs thought this woman, seeing the scars on Dervs's face, probably felt sorry for her. "I don't think so," she said.

"I can see things," replied the woman. "You have light around you."

Dervs looked up at the woman, trying to take in the kind of person who saw angels. The woman appeared to be in her forties, not thin, not heavy, dressed in jeans, a beige sweater and a suede jacket. Her hair was like the rest of her, nothing to distinguish it: medium length, brown.

"I know you don't believe me," the woman said, "but you should. I can see these things. You are giving off light. It's all around you."

She turned around with grace and walked out the door.

When Dervs's hair stylist was ready for her, Dervs

asked whether there was a woman haunting the salon, coming in, saying peculiar things to customers in the lounge area.

"Not that I'm aware of," said the stylist.

Like the wind, then, thought Dervs, this woman blew in and blew out, leaving the dried leaves of a thought — like Boreas, the purple-winged god of the north wind, whose two sons, the Boreades, chased away the Harpies plaguing King Phineus of Thrace. These Harpies stole Phineus's food each time he attempted to eat and were causing him to starve.

I cannot pretend to understand this, but I feel certain that all the people praying for Arthur, holding him in their thoughts, have contributed to his survival. I am not religious, and yet I believe this to be true. A couple weeks ago, Arthur received at least twenty cards from the Mt. Ennon Baptist Church in Clinton, Maryland.

He opened card after card, each with a signature he didn't recognize and "Mt. Ennon Baptist Church" written underneath.

"I don't know who these people are. Do you know them?" he asked me.

"I don't, but I can find out."

A little investigation revealed that the card senders were members of the church that Barbara Reeves, Arthur's D.C. office manager, attends. Barbara asked them to send cards letting him know they were including him in their prayers. There have been a number of occurrences like this that lead me to believe there are levels of connections between people we don't understand. But I think, under the right circumstances, we figure out how to push them into action.

So far Arthur has received over three hundred get-well cards. Truly. And twenty-four different flower bouquets, three cookie arrangements, and a gift basket packed with the foods I love to eat but wouldn't buy. Fifteen members of the Oregon Trial Lawyers Association gave blood for him in Portland. He's had trees planted in his name in Israel and contributions given to the Cystic Fibrosis Foundation.

Right now I feel as if we can use all the help anyone is willing to offer. Both Wally and Arthur are decompressing around me. Wally comes home from school today and bursts out crying because he hasn't eaten much of his lunch and he doesn't want me to be mad at him. Then he goes into his bedroom, and while he's trying to pull down the window shade, he yanks it off the wall instead. After about ten minutes, we tack a sheet up to cover the window. Wally eats dinner, does his homework, takes a bath, and is calm by the time he gets into bed. Wolfie and Big Bear talk to him. We read a story, and he settles into the pillows for the night.

At nine o'clock the phone rings. I check the machine and see that it's Arthur. I am so tired that I decide to ignore it. At 9:30, it rings again.

"Hey, Honey," Arthur says. "I just needed to talk to you."

He starts to cry.

"What's the matter?"

"I'm afraid about this operation tomorrow. It sounds so complicated, and I'm worried that something will go wrong. I feel like I'm settled here at Kentfield, and I don't want to go back to John Muir and have to stay there. Mostly I miss you and Wally. I feel so alone."

I'm sitting on the bed, watching two dots on the clock blink — on, off, on, off, on, off. I want the man on the other end of the phone to go away, go to sleep, shut down.

"Arthur, I'm sorry. I know how hard it has to be. I

want to say that you're not alone — and you're not — but there is no one there with you, and so you are."

"I hate this. I hate this so much," he says, still crying.

"I know you do. I wish I could be there to hold you."

"That's all I want. I just want you to hold me," he says. Then, "It's *not* all I want. I want all this to go away. I want to go back in time and have this not happen."

"I know. So do I. But we can't. Listen, that operation tomorrow. I know they're doing a lot and that it's scary, but you have two great surgeons. You will be fine, and this will let you begin walking."

Arthur will be taken by ambulance to John Muir tomorrow morning. Chris Coufal is going to attach an Ilizarov apparatus to Arthur's right calf, to keep the bones from moving while they reattach. This metal cage with bolts going from it to the patient's bones is an external fixator. After it is on, Arthur should be able to start physical therapy, so he can walk. In addition to the fixator, Dr. Coufal will be putting a metal pin in Arthur's big toe and Dr. Wyzykowski is going to do more rebuilding inside Arthur's right hand.

"I don't feel like I'm ever going to walk," says Arthur. "I've been lying in a bed for two months, and it doesn't feel like I'll ever get out. This is never going to end."

"Yes, it will," I say. "This will end, and you will walk, and you will get out of the hospital and go back to work, and we will have a normal life. It won't be the same as our old life; it will be different, but we will have normal days where we get up, Wally goes to school, we go to work. We will eat dinner together, go to the movies. You have to believe that. If you don't believe that, we are lost."

"I know. And I believe it. It's just that sometimes it's so hard to hold onto anything, and I'm just so tired of being alone."

"Me too," I say. "I'll see you tomorrow after the operation. You'll be fine, and Dr. Coufal says you'll only have to stay at John Muir for four or five days, and then they'll take you back to Kentfield. You have to hold onto knowing that Wally and I are always with you."

"I know," he says. "Good night. I love you."

"I love you too."

Instead of hanging up the phone, I want to turn it into a missile that will seek out Christopher Adney and split his head in two. I want to pull off all his skin and throw salt on him. I want a fire that he can never extinguish to burn in his gut. I want him to swim forever in a vat of boiling goats' blood. I want him to have pustules on his penis, never to have another hard-on, to be repulsive to all. I want his hair to fall out and putrid scales to grow in its place. I want him to smell like fermenting cabbage. I want him to take on the spirit and persona of a Hieronymus Bosch monster. I want him to be locked in a violent prison, to be raped nightly, to never sleep. I want him in misery for the rest of his life.

I am no angel.

I am walking up the stairs to Charlotte's office behind a woman who is wearing black and white horizontally striped leggings, like the Wicked Witch of the East, her striped legs sticking out from under Dorothy's house, ruby slippers at the end of them. The woman must be one of the therapists in the group with its office across the hall from Charlotte's. Sure enough, at the top of the stairs, she turns and unlocks the door on the left. I wait and then enter the code for the door on the right.

"I just walked up the stairs behind the Wicked Witch," I tell Charlotte. "Fortunately, she was a therapist from across the hall."

"You know, you're going to have to let me be the Wicked Witch sometimes," says Charlotte. "You sent her into the other office, but she wanted to come in here. I can handle her."

*What the heck is Charlotte off on now? I'm missing her witch reference. There she sits in her neat little suit with her tidy hair and perfect composure and I'm supposed to put the witch in her. Give me a fucking break. All I need her to do is put Band-Aids on my days, so I can get through them.*

"Here's the thing: I'm not following you about the witch, but I can tell you about a TV commercial. Is that close enough to a witch for you?"

"Whatever you want to say," responds the composed, tidy person.

"In 1982, I watched the CLIO Reel. Do you know what that is?"

"You'll have to tell me."

"It's a compilation of the best TV commercials of the year, the ones that have won CLIO Awards. I don't know who gives them, but this reel contained U.S. and international winners."

"Go on," Charlotte says.

"I was watching the commercials with some friends, and lots of the ads were funny, some were really clever. Anyway, I was enjoying this reel when an ad came on with no sound track, no sound at all, beginning to end, no sound. It opened with a close-up of a woman's head and shoulders, beautiful woman. She was wearing a white fur hat and coat, and she had pulled up the collar of her coat so it protected the bottom half of her face. All you could see were her nose, cheeks, and eyes. The camera stayed on a still shot of her for what seemed like ten seconds, a long time. Then the shot changed and now you were looking down onto a white beach as if you were standing on a cliff above it. Some black spots entered the scene, but the shot was too far away to make out what they were. As the camera moved in closer, you could see they were hunters. They were beating white baby seals with clubs. The camera angle remained static for another ten seconds — hunters and seals, the clubs moving up and down. Then the woman's face filled the screen again. This time she pulled down her collar, so you could see her mouth and the red lipstick brightening it. And then she smiled, this gorgeous woman in white fur. And when she opened her mouth, she revealed her fangs."

I tell Charlotte that the piece was produced by a Finnish agency for a group called Nature Conservation. It was titled *Vampire*.

"You want to know why I remember the commercial?" I say. "I was shocked when I saw it, not as much by the seals being bludgeoned to death as by the woman. She was my mother. I recognized my mother in this woman. You want the fucking witch in the room? She's here."

SIDESHOW

On tiny patent leather shoes the fat lady balances.
Her toes kiss the dirt as she sits spread
voluminous-legged on a cranky wood chair.
Don't you want to grab puffs of her flesh,
roll them in your hands for texture?

A woman like this doesn't disappear
and if she did, those hot kisses would last,
forever imprinted on the sideshow dust.
Kisses forever — the dream of children
jettisoned, ballooned by their mothers,

sent off with nothing to where life becomes
all levels of people visiting back and forth —
the queen from zone five to the lion-faced twins —
crossing time and places, where a shot
to the head with a spike heel means being noticed.

Come to the sideshow now. Become a hologram
under glass, jumping rope in perpetual
motion, as if swiping at flies

that circle your head. You are etched
with a hologram tattoo — Tiger Jimmy

shimmering one fine layer above your skin,
whispering *tell her to give it back to you.*
Or you ride a Harley to the deaf end of a drive-in
where all pictures and no words spell
the precision of your travels without

*Mother, I love you.* The fat lady opens
her arms wide, offers a nipple from which to suck
your geography. The result is her edges riffle,
you leave a child, and it is impossible to tell
where the body begins and where it ends.

Arthur is back at Kentfield following his operations. Wally and I are going over to have Thanksgiving dinner with him. I will take the meal — no turkey involved — only what I can pack up and not have to heat. We will have bread and cheese, herbed chicken breasts, salads, and a tarte tatin — all from a specialty grocery near Charlotte's office, a splurge, but this is a holiday. I stuff the food and drinks and plates and utensils into grocery bags, trying to remember everything we might need to make this festive.

Wally helps me load the bags into the car, and then we lift in his BMX bike, helmet, and pads, so he can show Arthur the tricks he has been working on. We feel pretty happy on the drive over and when we get to Arthur's room, he is clean-shaven, has had a haircut, and is eager to head out to the courtyard to celebrate the day. I have gotten good at helping him with transfers — getting him from the bed to his wheelchair, so we are motoring in minutes.

This day is a reason people live in the Bay Area. The light is rich and golden, the temperature about seventy degrees. Arthur and I sit in the sun and hold hands, he in his wheelchair, I at a picnic table next to him, while Wally rides his bike in the yard and up and down a ramp. He is performing for his father.

Arthur looks at me with his eye wide open — the left eye is still patched and will remain so for we don't know how long.

"Is this safe?" he says.

"It doesn't look that way to me," I say, "but his therapist says we have to grit our teeth and let him to do this, that it's his way of breaking free of the accident."

"That's one of us then," says Arthur. "You remember that I start physical therapy tomorrow, to learn how to walk again."

"Yes, it would be hard to forget that. You worried?"

"Sure, I'm worried. I have no idea if these legs are going to work, if all the metal in them is actually going to support my weight or if it's just stuff to keep my muscles from stringing together, turning into muscle knots."

"Yeah, like balls of yarn. Sorry. They'll work. This isn't the first time rods have been used to hold bones together. You should be excited. The sooner you get up, the sooner you get out," I say, watching Wally whiz by, standing on the bicycle seat, waving at us.

Arthur tells me that his goal is to get home by Christmas — "but they tell me I have to be able to do stairs before they'll release me. It's hard to think about walking up steps when I haven't even stepped on my legs yet."

"You will," I say.

He has spent the required three months lying in bed, so all the bones and rods and muscles should be knitted together. They should have formed some little communities by now.

"You'll be great," I add.

"Yeah, I just have to keep believing that. But, you know what? I'm happy to have today. I feel like we're basking, even if it's only for a moment."

"Basking is good. How about some pie?"

I think pie makes everything better. Pie and sun. I decide not to tell Arthur that his workers' comp insurance company has turned down our claim, saying that he was not working, but on vacation when we were hit. They will make us go to court. Getting this insurance to help cover Arthur's medical expenses is important. Since Mr. Adney had no insurance, we didn't get a penny from him. Today we won't discuss that. Today we are joyful.

The procedure is the same each time. Wally spends his first ten minutes with the respiratory therapist, Kris Cross, the woman who found Dr. Coufal, Arthur's orthopedic surgeon. Kris measures Wally's height and weight and tests his lung functions. This time she uses the three pigs screen to test. Wally is hooked up to a breathing tube, which is hooked up to the computer. He has to exhale as hard as he can into a mouthpiece. The strength and length of this exhalation enable him to blow down the pigs' houses — one-two-three — as if he were the Big Bad Wolf. Wolfie and I cheer as two houses fall, but after several tries, Wally can't blow down the third.

We leave Kris and go into an exam room to wait for the pediatric pulmonologist, John McQuitty, our trim and smiling expert on cystic fibrosis. He asks how everything is going, and I tell him about Arthur beginning to walk again. He shakes his head, as if the story makes him want to clear away spiderwebs. Then he looks straight at me, and his smile fades.

"Listen," he says, "Wally's pulmonary functions are down for the first time, and they are down substantially. I think he would be best served by getting him on intravenous antibiotics to clear out his lungs. And I need to put him in the hospital to do that. It would be for a week or two."

I have the strangest sensation in my face, as if ice water has been shot under the skin. My face is frozen, but then the process reverses and it heats up and begins to slide off the bones. I can feel my face sliding off, and the sliding mouth is wordless, empty. I'm trying to think, but everything is a jumble, as if my brain is sliding away too, trying to catch up to my face. I reach to grab a thought. All I come up with is *NO*. There has to be another way. I can't drive to Kentfield to see Arthur during the day and spend the rest of my time, including my nights, in San Francisco with Wally. I can't leave Wally alone in the hospital at any time. This is outside the boundaries of what is possible. I can't leave Arthur by himself for two weeks, especially when he's trying to walk.

"Is there any other way? Anything else we can do to try to get his lung function up?" I ask.

"You could try doing some advanced therapy at home. It would involve a lot more work, and you'd have to be absolutely diligent. And even if you were, I can't guarantee it would work. It probably won't."

"Give me a percentage," I say.

"Okay, there is maybe a ninety percent chance this won't work — so a ten percent chance you can do this at home," says John. "But if you want to try, I'll tell you what you need to do, and I'll give it two weeks. If his functions aren't up significantly, we'll have to put Wally in the hospital — to keep him healthy."

"Ten percent is better than nothing," I say. "It's better than the chances they gave Arthur for staying alive."

I look at John, trying not to cry as my insides collapse. Then I look at Wally, working my mouth into a shape I hope resembles a smile.

"We can do this, Wally, can't we? We can give it our best shot, right?"

Wally is holding onto Wolfie, understanding the emotion if not the words of the moment.

"Okay, Mom."

For the next two weeks, morning and night, Wally and I sit next to each other on the sofa as he inhales new antibiotics through his nebulizer. He hates the taste of the gentamicin but hangs in there with his inhales, working to get the medicine into his lungs. Wolfie and Big Bear are the cheering section — "Breathe, Wally, Breathe!" — as I envision killer molecules knocking out bacteria, fighter-plane molecules diving into the small airways, clearing pathways of the enemy, big hunker molecules exploding bacteria-ridden mucous hotels. We are good and faithful soldiers.

In two weeks, we go back to see John McQuitty. Kris runs a new set of pulmonary function tests. Wally and Wolfie and I are in one of the exam rooms waiting, when John walks in with a serious look on his face.

*Oh, shit,* I think. *Oh, shit.*

He looks me straight in the eye and says, "I don't know how you did this, but Wally's lung functions have all gone up. We'll have to keep an eye on him, have him come back in a month, but he's in great shape. I didn't believe it was possible; you know that, but you did it."

"We did it together," I say. "Wally and I, every day. He did the work. I was just the cheering section."

"I don't think you know how extraordinary this is," says John.

Other good news comes from Rona Silkiss, the eye specialist I have been seeing. She tells me that my left eyelid is healing so well, I might not even need a skin graft. I will have to continue gooping my eye with gel at night because it still doesn't close all the way. She also tells me that the seventh nerve above my left eyebrow will come back, that nerves take from six months to a year, or even longer, to heal. I will eventually be able to move that eyebrow again, the eyebrow with the slit through it.

On the downside, I'm still having temperature fluctuations. Since the accident, it feels as if my body's thermostat can't settle on a temperature. I get hot; I get cold. This seems to be related to sudden changes in temperature, emotional spikes, and lying down or getting up. I was told at St. Charles that this symptom often accompanies a head injury.

I've been driving these raw chickens around in my car, and I can't figure out why I forget to take them out. I bought them a day ago to make soup, and I can't remember to take them out of the car. When will they start to stink? I think they are somehow related to Arthur crying all the time and that the gynecologist wants me to get blood work. This is the first time since the accident that I've had a chance to check about this ovarian cyst. I tried to meet with Amy Huibonhua, my regular doc, but her office said she was booked and I couldn't get in for months, so I saw Dr. Yuan, who says she can't feel any mass and thinks I might be going through perimenopause. She ordered a blood test to check my estrogen levels and wants St. Charles to fax her their report on the cyst.

I worry about Arthur coming home, worry that I won't be able to take care of him. We are both physically exhausted and also exhausted by not being together. I want a vacation. I want some other things too:

I want Arthur to stop crying.

I want him to stop saying I'm putting pressure on him to walk.

I want to stop putting pressure on him to walk.

I want to stop running at top speed just to get things done every day.

I want to stop having to go to the hospital every day.

I want company.

I want not to want to kill myself.

## LUG THOSE LEGS

From John McQuitty's office, drive on Ygnacio Valley Road toward Highway 24/Oakland. Pass through the Caldecott Tunnel and stay on 24 to 80 toward Sacramento, veering right onto 580 West across the San Francisco Bay on the Richmond–San Raphael Bridge. Take the Sir Francis Drake Boulevard exit and merge into traffic. Keep going for about three and a half miles until you reach the Kentfield Rehabilitation Hospital, where Hans, the physical therapist, is trying to get Arthur up and walking for the first time since August.

Before we go in, you have to understand that Arthur has always thought of himself as an athlete. He played tennis and basketball in high school and was on his college basketball team, even though it was just Swarthmore. He's had sports injuries that kept him off his feet: torn ligaments and cartilage in his knee, broken ankle, broken toe. The man thinks he has experienced what it feels like to not be able to walk and then have to start over again using crutches. In addition, he's been doing lots of exercises in bed to build up strength. He can make transfers into and out of a wheelchair. The only thing he hasn't done in more than three months is to bear the weight of his body, now reduced by thirty pounds, on his legs. But, you know, he feels like himself, so he is sure it will be okay.

Once we're inside, you can see that Hans already

has Arthur in the physical therapy room, where Arthur is ready to move from his wheelchair up onto the parallel bars that will support him, one arm on each bar, as he will try to walk between them. Hans is on one side, his assistant on the other, so they can grab Arthur if he falters.

"Are you ready?" Hans asks.

"As ready as I can be."

"Then let's go."

And up he rises, standing now, on legs whose bone has been replaced by metal rods, legs of different lengths — the right an inch and a half longer than the left, to be repaired later—on new legs that have not previously been vertical with a body balanced on them.

Arthur is anticipating euphoria, balloons floating to the heavens, a chorus of trumpets. He has been waiting for this moment as the first step toward going home. He is excited and nervous. And scared. Really scared. Because once he is up, he realizes that these legs are not his. He cannot even feel them. They are some alien notion of legs, some Frankenstein patchwork of legs, legs that have no memory of ever having walked before, legs that have no feeling at all.

Where are his legs? Why can't he feel them? He tries a step, then another, then he starts to fall. Hans whisks the wheelchair in behind him, and Arthur plops into it. Shaking.

This is the most stunning moment that Arthur will experience in his entire rehabilitation process. These things attached to him don't feel like his legs. They don't feel like legs at all. They feel like disembodied stumps to which his body is somehow joined. It is shocking him and scaring him because now his body doesn't feel like it is his. He didn't expect this. All his life, his body has been his friend. He was agile, moved well, was a dancer. He was connected to his body, and to stand on his legs and not feel them, not even know how to move them, is more frightening because he has never imagined, has never known anything like this. Arthur realizes that he is going to have to get to know these legs, make the connection to them, make them his. Here's what he's decided he has to do: stand up, balance, lug one leg forward, balance, lug the other leg forward. He will *be* Frankenstein's monster. Whatever he will have to do to make a forward motion is not walking. This will not be like any physical activity he has ever experienced.

And right now, he is afraid to ever get back up on these legs again. He is afraid if he missteps, he could break another bone. He is afraid to break anything else in this unknown body. Our hero is utterly disoriented. And Dervs is not with him. He is alone in a room with these legs, alone in this hospital, this town, alone on this planet, a stranger even to himself.

ARTHUR IS COMING HOME ON THE 21ST. Yes, that is me shouting. Confirmed. Certain. He is coming home. All three of us are eager and frightened. And we have work to do to get ready. Today after Charlotte buzzes me in and I settle myself, I start to dump my fears that Arthur is going to take up all the space. As much as I want him near me, I fear that his needs are going to be larger than our house.

"That's what I get growing up with a mother whose needs were bigger than the universe," I tell her.

"What do you mean by that?" says Charlotte.

"Once, when I was fourteen, my mother and I walked to a nearby field where a carnival had set up for the week. This is one of two times I remember my mother going anywhere with me on a weeknight. The other time we went sledding. But this was summer and we went to gawk at the carnies, to eat dinner. My father worked shifts in a steel mill. He was working the middle shift this night — three to eleven. I was wearing shorts; my mother had on capri pants, what she called pedal pushers, although I never understood that, and as we were walking home we passed a row of high school guys sitting on a wall. They started to whistle and do the 'Hey, girlie' call that made me think I would rather eat eyeballs than look at them. When we had passed, my mother said to me, 'You think they were whistling at you? You're wrong. They were whistling at me.' I was fourteen; she was forty-two."

"She needed to believe the attention was for her," says Charlotte. "Do you remember what you thought about that at the time?"

"I know you hate it when I say this, but I don't know. I probably just took it as being my mother."

"She had trouble giving you anything, any emotional sustenance, so you learned not to expect any."

"I suppose. I also suppose that she didn't get attention when she was a kid, except maybe the negative kind. She used to tell me over and over how poor her family was, how her father was alcoholic and she would hear her mother crying on paydays and then my mother would have to go drag her father out of a bar and plead with him to come home. All that, but I think she loved him more than she ever loved anyone else."

"Why do you think that?" Charlotte asks me.

"Just the way she talked about him. Her only good memories of childhood involved her father. He used to make a game where he chased her around the table. He taught her how to play the piano. He was a musician, had a band in Atlantic City. I also think my mother was jealous of her four older brothers because he taught them to play wind instruments, but not her. And I think he was the source of her craziness. My best guess is that he was bipolar and drank to self-medicate. One of my mother's brothers did the same thing; another one was institutionalized for a while — a real family affair.

"Other than that, she had stories about begging people for food, having just one dress. She told me something that made her really mad was when she would say to her mother, 'I'm hungry.' And my grandmother would answer, 'Lick salt; you'll be thirsty.'

"She also had this story about a man once offering her a nickel if she would smell some clear liquid he had in a bottle. She said she took the nickel because it was a lot of money for her and she smelled the contents of the bottle. Turned out it was ammonia, and she ran home screaming. Ever after she believed the ammonia had burned out the nerves in her nose, claimed she could never smell after that. She had reasons to be needy. For sure she was mentally unstable, but I don't think that happened until she was twenty-one. My aunt told me that was how old my mother was 'when she got so mean.' That's how my aunt phrased it — 'she got so mean.' And you know what? I don't care. All the reasons in the world don't add up to it being okay for her to take her shit out on me."

"But we didn't start out talking about your mother. We started with Arthur, and I know you will resist hearing this, but you can't put your mother's neediness into Arthur," says Charlotte. "He is *not* your mother. He isn't trying to take anything away from you. That doesn't mean he won't need you, but you are allowed to need him too."

"Yeah, right."

*And what is it you need, Charlotte?*

Wally and I go to Kentfield early today. We want to be there in time for Arthur's morning physical therapy session. He's working on stairs now. This is the last piece of the getting-around-the-house puzzle, and Hans has saved them because they are so strenuous. We have two sets of stairs in our house that Arthur has to be able to manage. I will be there with him, but he has to do the grit of it.

Slow going. Arthur has to position himself so he can grab the stair railing with his left hand — his right hand and wrist are still healing from the reconstruction surgeries. I take his right crutch; he uses the left one for stability as he grabs the rail and places his right foot on the step, then hoists up his body. The left, stronger leg follows. He resists putting too much weight on his right leg, even though he weighs less than he used to. This reminds me of the short story "The Monkey's Paw." I have spent years trying to get Arthur to lose weight. Last spring, when I was training for a marathon, he finally got down to 180 pounds. Now he weighs 150. In W. W. Jacobs's story, a man wishes on a magical paw for money and gets it from insurance after his son is killed in a factory accident.

This is the first time in our eleven-year marriage that I've ever encouraged my husband to eat cheese steaks. Rikki found a place in San Francisco that makes a replica of a Philly cheese steak, with a semblance to what we grew up with, so she brings one to the hospital when she can. This restaurant also sells that Pennsylvania-kid favorite, the chocolate Tastykake. I used to love the chewy, brown cake covered with the thick strip of greasy icing. I haven't eaten one in years, but Arthur dives into each one that Rikki brings.

At this moment, however, he's diving into stairs, diving into getting down them, actually hoping he won't *be* diving down them. Instead of heaving his body up, he is trying to hold it back, keeping himself tilted so he doesn't tumble downward. He is terrified of falling, of needing one additional repair. The patch over his left eye exacerbates the process. His perspective is entirely different from what it used to be; you might even say he's lost it. In an attempt to get his eyes to track together and correct his double vision, an ophthalmologist injected his left eyeball with Botox to paralyze the muscles, so the eye can stay in one place and heal, they hope. He was awake when she did it, his eye open as the needle was inserted — a needle instead of a razor à la Luis Bunuel and Salvador Dali's surrealist film *Un Chien Andalou.* We're waiting to see if the injection will resolve the problem. Until it does, the eye patch stays and Arthur's perspective remains one-sided.

This is it — the end and the beginning. The day Arthur comes home. Almost four months after that day we were driving home from Oregon.

Wally and I are up and out of the house by 8:30 a.m., both of us excited and anxious. I realize that tonight, for the first time in four months, we will all sleep in the same place, in our home together. I also know that we are each different from the last time we all slept in our house together.

This is another sparkling day — sun bursting off the bay. Here is another reason to live in the Bay Area: If you have to take someone home from the hospital in December, you have a good chance the day will be a clear, blissful sixty degrees. I finished most of the hospital paperwork yesterday, so I only have a couple forms left to sign. My job now is to get Arthur from his room to the car — the new Volvo station wagon he hasn't yet been in — and to get him home safely.

I park the car near the exit door closest to Arthur's room. By the time we get to him, he is dressed and smiling. I took most of his clothing and room adornments home yesterday, so it doesn't take much to get the rest of his belongings loaded. I have to have room for both a wheelchair and crutches in the back of the car. Because his right hand was so badly damaged and is still healing from the last operation, Arthur has one regular crutch and one that is called a platform crutch. Instead of putting the crutch under his arm and taking hold of the crossbar with his hand, his forearm rests on a platform and the crutch is strapped to his arm with Velcro. This makes the process of getting onto and off the crutches more difficult. It is just one additional step in the transfer from wheelchair to crutches.

Arthur's hospital room has a burgundy sofa along the same wall as the door. When you stand in the room looking at the doorway, the sofa is to your left, and that's where Wally is standing while we get Arthur ready to roll out. The wheelchair is right inside the doorway, Arthur is facing me, his back to the door, getting ready to sit down in the wheelchair and give me his crutches. I am holding his left arm to give him support. Our eagerness to leave is palpable.

"Okay," he says. "Let's get out of here."

He begins to lower himself slowly into the wheelchair, and just as he does, I see the patient we call "Yeller" come screaming down the hall in his wheelchair, heading straight for us. Yeller has suffered a serious head injury and is generally watched carefully because his behavior is erratic, disruptive, and at times dangerous. He is always trying to get away from the nurses and other staff and yells at everyone for everything. I think, *Oh my god, he's escaped, keep him away.* And as I'm watching, he wheels up to Arthur's chair and yanks it away, screaming, "You don't need that chair!" The wheelchair goes spinning out of the room and into the hall. Instead of the wheelchair, it's now Yeller right behind Arthur, blathering.

I begin to pull Arthur up by his left arm, saying, "It's

okay. I have you." Arthur can't tell what's going on, but he senses the chair isn't there and he hears Yeller screaming, and he's off balance, trying to keep himself from falling. "I have you. I have you!" I repeat this louder and louder. But Arthur isn't processing. He throws his right arm up, swinging his crutch. I think his instinct is to try to swat the man behind him. But his crutch arcs wildly through the air and hits Wally, who falls onto the sofa and starts screaming too.

Now Arthur is yelling, "Get him out of here! Get him the fuck away from me!"

Four staff members come running at once. Two of them corral Yeller, the other two get behind Arthur, who, by now, is almost crying. I am holding him up, and he wants to get control of his right crutch. The nurses get his wheelchair from the hall, and we lower him into it. I go over to Wally, who is still crying, and I sit on the sofa to hold him, trying to explain what just happened and why Daddy was so upset by it. As I talk, I'm trying to understand it myself. This Arthur is one neither of us has ever seen — this is one who screams, whose emotions are a scratch beneath the surface, who yells *fuck* in front of his son. Wally and I sit holding onto each other while the Arthur we don't know berates the staff about how they allowed this to happen.

I want to leave. I want to leave and never see the inside of another hospital — even this one that has been wonderful until this moment. I want to get as much distance between me and any hospital as possible.

Wally and I get up, the nurse turns Arthur's wheelchair

around, and we all walk out into the day. I stow Arthur's crutches in the back of the car, the nurse helps him out of the wheelchair and into the car, then I collapse the chair and put it in the back as well. I take a deep breath before getting into the driver's seat. This is Arthur's first ride in a car since the accident. I am trying to behave as I imagine a cheerleader would, although I have never been a cheerleader, so I have trouble with that peppy confidence. Mostly, I want to ignore what just happened and to drive as carefully as I am able. Arthur does not speak, and neither does Wally, as I maneuver the car out onto the street.

The ride home takes forty-five minutes on a good day, and this is a good day, although none of us says much. We are each just trying to get through it, still agitated as a result of our departure. We drive out of Marin, across the Richmond–San Rafael Bridge. The bay is still chopping up the sun, and we can see Alcatraz Island and San Francisco off to the right. This seems to calm us as we drive south on Interstate 80 to 580 to 24 to 13. I hold onto each turn as it takes us closer to home and the time I can get Arthur out of the car. He is sitting back as if he is frozen solid; I can feel his fear. Once he tells me to slow down. I am only going 45 mph on the freeway, the slowest car on the road. I want to slow down and speed up at the same time. I want to get up the hill to our house and pull into the driveway, and then I want to walk up into the East Bay hills for about six miles, so someone else — I have no idea who — will have to take care of Arthur, get him out of the car and down the stairs and seated, so he can breathe without fear.

The incident with Yeller puts into relief new differences between Arthur and me. In our prior lives, I would have been furious and Arthur would have tried to make a joke, keep everyone calm. In these new incarnations, Arthur is livid, angry beyond reasoning. The idea that someone would pull a chair out from under him has become life-threatening. Chair-pulling, however, was the name of my mother's game. It appears that now Arthur and I have the same fear, having arrived at it on such different paths.

Of course, I was not my mother's only victim. One year for Christmas she bought my father a single-lens reflex camera he had wanted for years. He set about experimenting with f-stops, shutter and film speeds, depth of field. But he never took his pictures fast enough: "What are you doing? Inventing the camera? I can't stand like this forever. It can't be that hard to figure out how to take a photograph, a monkey could do it." And he didn't take them well enough: "You got shots this good with that little camera you used to have. I guess your eye hasn't gotten any better." In July my father put the camera away, and then my mother ridiculed him for giving up. When I was in my twenties, my mother safely dead, my father got out the camera again, but only to give it to me. He told me he could no longer find joy in photography.

I come back to this reality as I pull into our driveway. As we set about getting Arthur out of the car and down the stairs to our house, I want to rewind the morning and start over, so we can make a flawless exit from Kentfield with nurses in 1950s uniforms waving flowers and smiling, wishing us well on our journey to recovery, which, they are sure, will be short. Patients and staff band together in a chorus singing "Cross Over the Bridge." I want hope, not desperation, to be walking into the house with us.

Our friends Ann and Steve and Amy and James and Curtis and Cameron are coming over for dinner tonight. We are making what has become a New Year's Eve tradition, a Joe's stone crab dinner: crabs flown in on dry ice from Joe's Restaurant in Miami, creamed spinach, Armand salad, hash browns, and key lime pie. Amy is from Miami Beach, and James produced the cookbook for Joe's Stone Crab Restaurant. They introduced us all to this yearly feast, and James takes over lots of the cooking. Ann makes caviar pie. We serve icy martinis. The combination is heavenly.

I don't drink this year because of the head injury injunction against it, but the night is glorious anyway. There is no disco ball, yet light seems to spin around the room, flickering in corners, exposing nothing — no hidden cockatrix, no kraken, no zombie, no fury, no harpy. The room glows and we are all a little giddy — to have Arthur at home and speaking cohesively. He is even able to get around a little bit. This feels like the beginning of the crawl back to our lives. We toast our health, our friends, our lives — to 2003 being a grand year all around.

Arthur wakes up about nine o'clock this morning, complaining of serious pain at one of the pin sites on his right leg. A pin site is where the screw from his external fixator enters his leg, the screw essentially extending from the metal frame of the fixator through the flesh into his bone. The Ilizarov apparatus is designed to help ensure that the bone heals correctly. I'd seen them before on people who had neck surgery; somebody called it a halo, but it looks to me like a tomato cage surrounding, in this case, Arthur's lower leg. Arthur says the pain is excruciating when he tries to bend his right ankle. I pay attention because he has not spoken about having pain in his legs except when I am cleaning out the pin sites. When I have to get into the sites with a Q-tip and antiseptic in the morning and at night, he grits his teeth and holds tight to a pillow.

Arthur lies on the bed while I put his shoes on him — first the left, then the right one with the front end cut off to accommodate the metal pins sticking out of his right toe. This shoe business is delicate; if I hit one of the toe pins, it will not only hurt, it could hold up the healing. His shoes have to go on every time Arthur gets out of bed, even before he can go to the bathroom, because he needs the extra support they give him. His pants go on after his shoes. Rikki bought him a couple pairs of athletic pants that open with snaps on the outsides all the way down both legs. Being able to open the pant leg works to accommodate the fixator and makes it much easier to get the pants on.

After his shoes are tied and pants are snapped, Arthur sits up by slowly swinging his legs over the side of the bed and then pushing up his torso. I hand him his crutches, he rises onto them, and navigates the ten steps to the bathroom. Our bedroom, on the lower level of the house, is set up so the toilet and shower are in their own room off one corner and the two sinks are along one wall in an alcove off the main part of the bedroom. I take the crutches as Arthur sits on the toilet. I close the door and leave. When he is ready, I hand back the crutches and help him up. He walks back to bed. From behind him, I can see how gingerly he treats his right foot. While his right foot was smashed, it was his left knee that has been rebuilt. Even though these injuries should be burned into my consciousness, sometimes I forget which side had what damage.

Arthur sits on the edge of the bed, and I take the crutches and come back with a glass of water and a Pepcid because ten years ago he had a bleeding ulcer and now has to take a daily acid-reducer. After asking him if he wants one, I also give him a Darvocet, which has been prescribed for pain. After he takes the pills, I take off his shoes and help him get his legs onto the bed and back under the covers. He falls asleep quickly, just at ten o'clock. It has taken us nearly an hour to do this. What we used to consider simple actions, or what we didn't used to think of at all, now have become exhausting activities, consuming time and energy and emotion.

At one o'clock I wake Arthur to get him up and washed and dressed in time to get him to a 3:15 appointment with Chris Coufal, his orthopedic surgeon. Arthur is groggy and looks pale. I'm thinking it's the Darvocet; he's sensitive to painkillers, which is why he tries not to use them. I get his shoes on, hand him the crutches, and walk with him to the bathroom. After he's finished, he manages to get back up on the crutches himself and stands at the door of the bathroom. I'm sitting on the bed reading, and when I look up I see that his face is ashen. He is sweating profusely. I run over and help him into the chair I have set up in front of the closest sink. I originally put it there so he could sit down while he was washing, shaving, and brushing his teeth. I am standing behind him and can see his grayish-white face in the mirror above the sink.

"I don't feel well," he says. "I'm really shaky and cold."

"Just sit here for a minute. See how it goes," I suggest. "We can always cancel the appointment with Coufal if you need to go back to sleep."

"Maybe it was the pain medicine," he says.

I begin to say something in response, but at that moment Arthur starts falling forward from the waist, his head aiming straight for the front edge of the sink. I look into the mirror at the same time that I catch him. His eyes are wide open. My arms are around his chest, holding him against the chair back. He is unconscious. I am afraid that he is dead.

I yell for Wally, who is playing upstairs.

"Wally! Come down here. Hurry up. I need you!"

Wally appears in the doorway in what feels like a

second. I say to him as calmly as I can, "Dial 911. Tell them we have a medical emergency."

Wally looks at me and at Arthur and screams. His mouth is wrenched open and a wailing noise is coming out. Loud, it is so loud. He is standing rooted to the spot with this banshee noise coming out of him.

"Wally, stop screaming!"

I am yelling now, so he hears me.

"Stop screaming," I say again. "I need you to call 911. I can't reach the telephone. You have to do it."

We don't have a portable phone in the bedroom. My old telephone from my house in Tucson is on Arthur's bedside table.

"Wally! Call 911!"

My heart is racing; I can't breathe. I can't let Arthur go; I can't get to the phone; my child is standing in the doorway screaming.

Wally looks at me and seems to register understanding. He picks up the phone and dials 911. He looks up and tells me it is not working.

"What do you mean not working? Just dial 911. They will answer."

"Mom, it's not working. The phone isn't working."

"Okay, then try to get the phone to me. It has a long cord. You will have to untangle it and drag the phone across the floor to me, so I can reach it. I can't let go of Daddy."

At this, Wally picks up the phone and throws it to me. It lands near enough so I can reach down and pick up the earpiece and receiver and dial. The phone is working fine.

I tell the operator my name and address.

"Is this a medical emergency?" she asks.

"Yes."

"I'll transfer you to medical."

The phone rings about ten times and a dispatcher answers. I give my information again and say, "My husband has passed out following problems with some orthopedic work. I'm holding him up in a chair so he doesn't fall over and hit his head."

"I'll send an ambulance right away."

I can hardly hear the dispatcher as she says this because Wally has run over to Arthur and is screaming in his ear, "Daddy! Don't die, Dad! Don't die!"

Wally can't stop. I can't hear. He screams over and over, "Daddy, don't die!"

And as if by just hearing Wally's voice inside his head, Arthur nods a little and moans. He twists his head around to look at Wally and says very quietly, "I'm all right."

But Wally can't stop screaming. As this is happening, the doorbell rings once, then again.

"Wally," I say, "Wally! Daddy is okay. He's okay. The ambulance is here. Can you open the door and bring them down here?"

Wally looks at me.

"Honey, go open the door and show them where we are."

Wally stares at me a little longer — his eyes are blank, stunned — and runs out of the room and up the stairs to open the door.

They have come quickly, a fire truck first because the station is only a mile down the hill, two men and a woman, the EMT. She walks right in and gets an oxygen monitor on Arthur, then a heart monitor. She starts an IV. I am by fast turns relieved to have them here and frantically trying to explain the situation. I am concerned about his heart. Arthur's father had a heart attack at age sixty-two, his grandfather at fifty. Even though Arthur is younger, I am worried.

"How is his heart?" I keep asking.

As the EMT begins directing operations and hooking up more equipment to Arthur, Wally runs across the room to the sliding doors that lead out onto the deck. He stands watching, with his fingers in his ears, so he won't have to hear. His face wears the same stunned expression as before; his eyes are open too wide.

Soon afterward, two more men come in. They are the ambulance crew. They get Arthur to the floor and are hooking him up to more monitors and screens.

"What's going on?" I ask. "Is there something wrong with his heart?"

An EMT finally tells me that Arthur's heart is working fine. They are on the phone with someone, feeding information. I want to ask if he is going to live, but I can't get that out, and I also can't figure out what could be wrong with him. There are too many choices. One of the EMTs asks me what hospital I want Arthur taken to.

"John Muir," I say. "That's where he was earlier and where his orthopedic surgeons practice and where they have his records."

One of the EMTs pulls me out of the room at this point and tells me that John Muir is in Contra Costa County and we are in Alameda County. He says they are one of only three ambulance crews working in Alameda County right now, and their supervisor wants them to stay close. John Muir is a forty-five-minute drive, through the Caldecott Tunnel. He tells me I have to make a decision — send them to John Muir for a long period of time or go to a closer hospital in Alameda County.

"Look, I don't want to jeopardize anyone's chance of getting an ambulance, but Arthur's case is so complicated that he needs to go where we have access to his records. He has to go to John Muir. Nobody else will know what his history is," I say.

"Okay," says the EMT, "that's where we'll go."

"Can we go with him in the ambulance?" I ask.

"Sorry, ma'am. We can't take children in the ambulance. You're going to have to drive separately. Your son is too young to go with us."

They're strapping Arthur into a chair to carry him up the two flights of stairs that lead to the street. Arthur is mostly out of it. Every so often his eyes open. He's trying to be helpful but doesn't seem to have a full grasp of the situation. It's as if he is partially conscious, flitting in and out of having a light on in his head. One of the firefighters pulls me aside and tells me I made the right decision about the hospital. I am so grateful to this man for saying that. I want to tell him how much his saying that means, but all I can manage is, "Thank you. I hope I am right."

As they work to get Arthur to the ambulance, I try to

think what I have to take with me: his crutches, some of his medicines — Darvocet, Pepcid, Ambien — long pants. My thoughts are flying around, bouncing off the interior of my skull, skittering too fast. A jacket. A book for me to read. I can't catch them. What am I going to do with Wally at the hospital? I can't catch even one of them. I have to *do* something.

"Wally, get your shoes on and a jacket and pick out some toys to take with us. I don't know how long we'll be at the hospital."

Wally is walking around in little circles.

"What's happening, Mom? What are they going to do to Dad?"

He is pulling on the edges of his sleeves, stretching the fabric down to cover his hands. His circles are making me dizzy.

"Can you stand still for just a minute, Honey?" I ask him.

We look at each other, and I think we see ourselves, our crazy selves, in the mirror that is the other. I throw on an extra shirt and a fleece vest. Wally says he needs to get Wolfie. I give him Arthur's jacket to carry.

While we are scurrying around gathering what we think we'll need, Arthur has been loaded into the ambulance. The driver tells me they are going to leave. I answer that we will be right behind. I look into the ambulance through the back doors and see Arthur and the EMT next to him. I want to say something to Arthur, yell some encouragement, tell him he is not alone, but nothing comes out of my mouth. I go to the driver's window and say, "Don't let him die in the ambulance."

"He's not going to die, ma'am. He's going to be all right," he says.

"Okay. Then I'll see you at the hospital," I say, and watch the driver maneuver out of the driveway.

"Let's get going, Wally," I say.

In spite of the driver's assurances, I have no faith that Arthur will survive the ride. Wally and I are both running. I grab my purse and my phone and hope I haven't forgotten anything. The thought that I ought to call someone to let them know what's going on enters my consciousness for a moment, but I sweep it away. All I can deal with now is getting in the car and driving as fast as possible to John Muir.

We are doing okay. I am trying to be calm. We go the back way to the tunnel and pick up some time. We are in the tunnel's far right bore and I can see the ambulance up ahead of us in the right lane. We are in the left. Each bore of the Caldecott has two lanes going in the same direction. Traffic is moving pretty well, about 25 mph, when I see brake lights up ahead. A lot of brake lights. Wally is listening to Radio Disney, so he isn't paying attention to anything else. Traffic ahead of me is stopped.

*This can't be happening. There can't be a stall in the tunnel.*

But there is. Nothing is moving. And this is the moment, this very one, in which all the anxieties and fears coalesce, this is the moment of all the terrible moments in this disaster so far, when I am crawling closest to insanity.

*I have to get out of this tunnel!*

I want to start screaming and scream and scream and scream and not stop for hours. I am going to be incoherent, institutionalized. My son will be re-traumatized, alone, neither parent functioning once again. I am going to lose it right here in the middle of this goddamn tunnel with all the built-up exhaust and red brake lights and dirt from millions of tires, all the impatient drivers who will not be kind to a screaming woman and her screaming son.

*Stop. Breathe. Find your defenses. Now is the time to pull them all out. You can't change the situation. Change yourself. Wally is in the backseat. You are not allowed to scream. You have to be calm. Breathe. Breathe. Start counting backward from one hundred in Russian. Do it! Breathe and count. Breathe and count.*

I am at forty-two when the lights ahead start to move. We have only been in the tunnel about five minutes, I guess. Or five lifetimes. Five centuries. Five sleepless nights. Five nightmares. Five leg surgeries. Five deaths.

And then we're out and driving fast on Highway 24 toward Walnut Creek. At least I know the way and where to park and how to navigate the hospital. This gives me confidence; I'm not traveling blind. And it is another spectacular day. I register the light, lemonade light, floating light, light filled with yellow sparkles. I appreciate it. It feels like light made just for me, just to keep me going.

We pull into the hospital parking lot as the ambulance pulls up to the emergency room doors. As we get out of the car and I start to look for Arthur's crutches, I realize that I forgot them. Wally and I run over to the ambulance; Arthur is already in a wheelchair. I am so grateful he's sitting up. He is groggy, disoriented. He tells me there is something wrong with his eye.

"My left eye hurts," he says.

"I thought it was your leg, Honey."

"Yes, my leg hurts. But there's something wrong with my eye too. It's not right."

"The doctors can look at that. Everything is going to be all right. We're at the hospital now. You'll be okay," I say.

*Can't there be just one damn thing wrong with him? Now he's whining about his eye. He should have stayed at Kentfield. At least they would know how to deal with him.*

The orthopedist orders X-rays, and after they come back concludes there is an infection at one of the pin sites. While this is going on, Arthur continues to complain about his eye. The orthopod sends for an ophthalmologist who, when he shows up, now early in the evening, says he doesn't really see anything unusual and tells me he isn't an expert in this area.

*What area is this? It's his eye, dipwad. How big a space is that? Aren't you an ophthalmologist?*

I'm talking to him about how Arthur's left eye doesn't track correctly and has limited movement and that he received a Botox shot. The doctor recommends that Arthur see another ophthalmologist — Rona Silkiss, the woman who has been treating my eyelid. Apparently she is the expert in eye trauma and eyelid injuries. However, when they try to locate Dr. Silkiss, it turns out she is on vacation and out of the country, and she won't be back in her office until Monday, January 6. Isn't there another doctor in the East Bay who can address this eye issue? No. I'm told Dr. Silkiss is the one we have to see, and they set up an appointment for us for Monday afternoon at one o'clock.

*Okay, we have to get through four days without this getting worse.*

By the time we are released, it is nearly seven o'clock. Arthur is allowed to come home. He has antibiotics and I have further instructions on cleaning the pin site on his leg. I am thankful that the emergency room personnel help me get Arthur to the car, since I don't have his crutches. I call Cherise, who had arrived with Geoff to pick up Wally about an hour after we got here; she tells me they are at California Pizza Kitchen having dinner, and they will meet us at home when they are finished. I am grateful that Arthur isn't worried about food or even hungry. The last thing I want to do is make him dinner.

After we get home, I get Arthur into bed right away. He is exhausted. When Wally and Cherise arrive, I get Wally doing his CF breathing and then into bed. I catch a couple minutes with Cherise to update her on the latest medical news, and after she leaves, I sit on the sofa thinking how nice a glass of wine will be. Then I remember that I can't drink. I am truly ready for a drug of some sort. The only one I can come up with is a huge caramel sundae. I've never been heavy into food as comfort, but when sex, drugs, and alcohol are out of the picture, this goopy melt of a mess is what's left.

"Love looks not with the eyes but with the mind"
— William Shakespeare
*A Midsummer Night's Dream*

For me, love looks neither with the eyes nor mind, but with a gut feeling. After we return home from John Muir, I think that we have resolved this latest setback and that we'll be able to deal with Arthur's eye on Monday when we see Rona Silkiss.

On Friday morning, however, Arthur says the pain in his eye is feeling more like there is a knife stuck in its center. We reassure ourselves with the knowledge of the Monday appointment and try to take it easy through the day. On Saturday morning, I wake up and look at Arthur and nearly pass out. His left eye has emerged from his head and is an eyeball at the end of a swollen blob of white, mucousy-looking material. I remember the actor Peter Lorre describing himself as having hard-boiled eyes and think this is an egg-white eye.

Or I am Gregor Samsa, but, instead of waking as a beetle, I wake to find a gigantic eye has taken up residence in my room. At first I think it is in the bed, but then I realize the eye has really settled on the floor and seems to be getting larger by the second until it is taking up almost all the space in the room. The eye has become a globe, the world, a map of the universe. How will I get around it? Is there room to walk? There is no room to walk; I can't move — the eye is everywhere. Like Gregor Samsa, my focus has moved from the everyday to an aspect of life that has taken over all others.

Arthur looks at me and says, "What's wrong?"

"Does your eye still hurt?" I ask.

"No more than it did yesterday."

This is where I try my best to have some still spot in my psyche and voice.

"I think we should go to the hospital. It looks a little worse," I tell him.

Before I get him out of bed, I call Rikki and ask her to please meet us at Alta Bates hospital in Berkeley, the closest one to us. I'm hoping that she will stay with me and Arthur and that my brother-in-law, Eric, will be available to take Wally off with their children, Moss and Emma. Rikki says they will meet us at the hospital, and I go about getting Arthur up and dressed and Wally dressed and fed. I'm running between our bedroom and the family room, where Wally is doing his vest treatment before we go.

At the hospital, no one really knows what to do with Arthur. They know there's a problem, but the mantra is, "He needs to see Dr. Silkiss." Until Monday, there isn't much to be done except keep Arthur quiet. They give me a medicinal gel to put on his eye, and at the end of the day, we go home.

That night I call Al and Marcia and ask them to come out. Whatever is going on, it feels like more than I can handle alone. They make arrangements to fly to Oakland tomorrow, January 5, so they can be here Monday for Arthur's appointments with Chris Coufal in the morning and Rona Silkiss in the afternoon. I try to explain to Wally that this is just another bump in the road and that his dad will be fine. For his part, Arthur *is* trying to be fine. He is much less freaked out by the way his eye looks than I am; perhaps that's because he can't see so well out of his other eye. He wants to know what's going on and whether it can be repaired.

I pick up Al and Marcia at the airport on Sunday, and on Monday morning, we all get up early and take Wally to school, so we can get to Chris Coufal's by 9:30 a.m. Since Arthur is wearing an eye patch, no one sees the eye pushed out of his head. Marcia has been good enough to put the medicine on the egg-white eye. She says the eye bothers her less than the metal pins coming out of Arthur's leg. While the blood at the pin sites on his leg doesn't bother *me*, the chemosis — crusting, hardening of the emerged eye white — is difficult for me to look at, let alone touch. It makes me want to barf.

After the Coufal appointment, we have lunch and go to Dr. Silkiss's office. The waiting room is crowded, and we are four people, so I spend some time outside. It takes about forty-five minutes for Arthur to get called in, and then another fifteen minutes in the examining room until we see the doctor. She is a slight, attractive, dark-haired woman who looks to be in her thirties and is very nice to us. She says she has some suspicions about what is going on with Arthur's eye and sends us across the street for a CT scan. After the scan we go back to her office, where we wait again. When we see her for the second time, she says Arthur has a *carotid-cavernous fistula* — translation: he has a hole in the carotid artery located in the cavernous sinus behind his eye, which is mostly fed by blood from the vein, as opposed to the artery. This has caused blood leaking from the artery to collect behind his eye, essentially pushing the eye out of the socket. In order for the eye to recede to its correct position, the hole has to be stopped up and the pooled blood reabsorbed. Dr. Silkiss has called the only team of doctors in California that operates on such anomalies, neurovascular interventional radiologists, who, luckily for us, practice in San Francisco. Arthur has an appointment tomorrow at UCSF hospital, the University of California hospital on Parnassus.

Following his appointment on Tuesday, where the UCSF team confirms Dr. Silkiss's finding, Arthur is scheduled for surgery on Friday, January 10. Before that happens, however, he has to go through his medical history and the informed consent. That takes place on Thursday, and I do not go. Al, Marcia, and Rikki all show up with Arthur for his appointment. I don't want to hear everything that could go wrong. The Bryant contingent can handle that.

When they return, Al tells me it took hours with the doctor to go over the host of problems that could occur as a result of this operation. He asks me if I want to know what they are. I tell him no. I will learn three years later that Rikki's biggest fear had been brain damage. I think loss of vision is possible, as is an embolism. At the moment, however, my unconscious is trying to figure out how to face the possibility of losing Arthur yet again. Consciously, I think of managing every detail of our lives except the eye.

Here's what this neurovascular interventional radiologist is going to do. He will insert a wire into Arthur's groin and thread it up an artery to the fistula, the hole in the artery behind Arthur's eye. At the end of the wire is a tiny balloon. When the doctor gets the balloon into exactly the right position, he will inflate the balloon to close the hole. In a perfect world, the balloon will stay in the perfect position and tissue will grow perfectly over it to close the hole. The balloon will eventually disintegrate, but the now-perfect artery doesn't need it any more. The pooling blood will become re-assimilated and Arthur's eye will go back to its former state, back into its orbit.

On Friday morning, Ann drives Arthur and Al and Marcia across the Bay Bridge to UCSF hospital. The operation is scheduled for ten o'clock. Al or Marcia will call me when it's over. They are going to stay in San Francisco with Arthur while I stay in the East Bay, taking care of Wally. If all goes well, Arthur will be able to come home Sunday, so it won't be that long a time.

Wally is in school. I am trying to work, trying to get words on a page. I've been writing a second volume of poetry and have made a couple attempts at a novel. Before the accident I was researching a book about chronic illness and how families deal with that pressure, but that has landed in a box in the closet. The only constant is that I am a faithful recorder of what happens in our lives. I have notebooks full of daily details; writing poems is beyond anything I can manage. Reading poetry, however, keeps me sane, gives me new ways of looking at the world — which I think is a big job of art. I grab the anti-poems of Nicanor Parra and get lost.

The phone rings at two o'clock. Marcia tells me the surgeon says everything went as well as could be expected. He was able to exercise the easiest option for getting the balloon into place. I leave shortly after her phone call to go pick up Wally from school and take him to see his therapist, Chris, over on Solano Avenue at the north end of Berkeley. While Wally is in with Chris, I walk up Solano and buy a truly hideous jacket: purple, green and brown rectangles — a jacket I will never wear. It's as if I am clothing someone not me, someone who wears blocks of colors or boxy jackets or purple skirts. My normal attire is dark solids, cut close to the body, so I can knife myself through groups and crowds without much notice.

Arthur, Wally, and I are again waiting for Arthur to be released from a hospital. We are in room 817 at UCSF, and the big excitement is football: the San Francisco–Tampa Bay playoff game. The 49ers are losing 31 to 6, and the crowd in this four-patient room is disappointed and complaining. The Raiders play at four o'clock in Oakland, and all I hope is that we get out of here soon and that there won't be too much traffic on the Bay Bridge.

Four beds, too many people. Arthur is fortunate to be by the window. The man in the next bed, whom Arthur says had been up yelling and agitated most of the night, has three visitors, two men and a woman whose voice sounds like that of actress Jennifer Tilly, a little-girl voice, a cartoon siren voice, a voice that doesn't seem real. The sounds coming from her remind me of the movie with Tilly and Gina Gershon, where the two of them murder Tilly's mobbed-up boyfriend and take off together with all his money. I can't think of the name of the film, but it was Betty Boop on downers, too sexy for any sound but "ooooooo." *Bound*, that's it.

We are waiting for the interventional radiologist on duty to come by, so he can release Arthur. And in the middle of a play that the 49ers are blowing, a man with long, dark hair, slicked back, in a black sweater and white lab coat appears. He's very handsome, and when he speaks I think he has an accent, maybe not; I can't be sure. This is all too much like a movie for me. The doctor gives Arthur a vision test, which Arthur passes, and he says if Arthur hears any whooshing in his head, that is a problem. My husband says he's never had whooshing in his head. Let's go home.

Taking a deep breath here before I say this: Arthur is driving me crazy. At 10:30 last night, when he was in bed and I was still in the living room, I heard him calling and calling for Marcia, who was already asleep in the guest room. She didn't hear him, and when I got to the bedroom, he said he was calling her so she could find whatever was ticking and keeping him awake. I told him I would look. I couldn't hear the ticking, but I figured since the rest of Arthur's body was now bionic, perhaps his ears were too. I checked inside drawers, in the closet, the bathroom. I checked the bedclothes; I checked for errant watches; I checked Wally's room. I couldn't find anything, so I told Arthur to take an Ambien, which I thought he did; however, he woke me at one, two, and three o'clock in the morning, each time turning on the light. At one, he needed to use the bathroom. At two, he wanted some Tylenol because either his eye or his leg hurt. At three, he decided he had to go upstairs because he said that I was snoring and he couldn't sleep.

Al and Marcia tell me they will stay for another week and two days. They have been here a week and a half already, and unlike fish and visitors that stink after three days, I am happy to have them here. Having Arthur home is a lot of work, and I can't seem to form a connection with him. He's speaking in his *head injury voice.*

I write that Arthur is driving me crazy, and I don't even feel guilty saying it anymore. I feel like he drove me into this accident; the accident drove me into therapy and the unwelcome blast of my mother; he drove me out of St. Charles too soon because he wasn't around to help take care of Wally. He is driving the train we are on now. And I want to get off. Is that saying too much?

I am curious about the committee that comes up with hospital interior designs. Here in pre-op the floor is grayish-white, the walls are beige, and the curtains are gray-green. Cold. Arthur is under lots of blankets and I am not sure if he is cold from the temperature or the austerity of color here. It doesn't matter too much, since he is asleep, giving Marcia and me a little time to talk about plates, serving dishes, glassware, knives.

The pre-op smells sweet; I wonder if Sallie put something on Arthur's hair yesterday when she helped him wash it. Sallie is his occupational therapist. She comes to our house three days a week and helps Arthur relearn how to take a shower, wash his hair, dress himself, given the restrictions of his new body. His physical therapist, Liz, comes five days a week. Both of these women walk in our door fresh and bright and smiling — every day. They are part of the John Muir Home Health Care system, and would not be available to us if we didn't have good health insurance. Nobody could afford what this accident has cost us.

Marcia and I brought Arthur here for the operation to remove his external fixator and the pins sticking out of his right toe. Both these devices have kept him from even attempting normal walking. I am twirling Arthur's wedding ring, which I wear on my ring finger held in place by my own ring. It took us so many years to get together. I hope this is the worst of the better-or-worse deal because I am still trying to find that guy I married, the one who was always joyous and positive and thought any good thing was possible for us as long as we wanted it together.

Our relationship coalesced in January of 1991 in Honolulu. Arthur and I were having dinner before we went dancing on the last night of our vacation together, a vacation we had taken as friends and which changed course midway.

Keo's Restaurant was redolent with smells of sa-tey shrimp, duck curry, Thai noodles with chicken. The walls were lined with posed photos of smiling celebrities showing way too many teeth, marking their passages through Keo's space. Tomorrow Arthur would return to work in Washington, D.C. The following day I would return to Tucson and my teaching job.

We would probably see each other again in six months, when I traveled east to teach for the summer. We would talk on the phone weekly as we have for several years. Up until now, our relationship has been platonic — ten years of impacted lust — because we wanted different lives: Arthur always knew he wanted children; I always knew I didn't. My parents left me no model for child-rearing, and I didn't think I was equipped to do it. That was the sticking point between us, more like a sticking obelisk, a sticking monument.

But this night I was wearing a perfect black dress that my friend Martha would later describe as the size of a postage stamp. Arthur bought me this dress on Maui, where we had spent most of the previous week, because I had fallen in love with it and would never have been able to afford it or willing to spend the money on it if I could. He sneaked away while I was at the beach and came back holding a large, gift-wrapped box containing this dress, the kind of dress that makes you feel sexy and insecure at the same time, a dress that calls attention to itself: here I am, a black spaghetti-strap body hugger!

I was grateful for all the hours I had spent playing tennis and hiking and doing aerobics, and at the same time I was worried that the dress was cut way too low and way too high.

Arthur and I were sitting at the table, finishing the last bits of mango with sticky rice, my favorite dessert, when words flew out of my mouth.

"You know how sometimes you think doors are closed in your life, and then you realize that maybe, given the right circumstances, you could open them," I said.

"Try English with me," said Arthur. "I'm a lawyer, not a poet."

"I've been thinking," I said, "that it might be all right to have kids together."

Arthur looked me dead in the eye and said, leaving a space between each word, "Do not fuck with me about this."

"I'm not."

This was the first moment in the years I had known him that Arthur had no witty comeback. He got up from the table and walked over to a wall filled with celebrity photos, appearing to study each one. I realized that he didn't know or care who those people were, but when he came back to the table, he said, "You've been thinking having kids together might be a good idea? What will it take for you to decide?"

"A little time," I said.

"Okay," he said. And that was the last we spoke of it that night. We finished the sticky rice, caught a cab, and went dancing.

The next morning was Sunday, and at breakfast, over newspapers, I said, "You know, there's a chance that I won't be able to get pregnant. You should know that."

"I already know that," Arthur said. "All those conversations we've had over the years—I was listening. And whether you can get pregnant or not isn't the most important thing. What is most important is that we both *want* the same thing. If we *want* the same thing, we can work out how we go about getting it—or not—but we are in it together."

## THE ORACLE FRACTURE

Dervs was talking to a friend in Washington, D.C., and told her that one of her injuries was an orbit fracture, shattered bones around her eye. But what her friend heard was that Dervs had an *oracle fracture*, and it turns out that is exactly what Dervs had.

Five years before they were married, Dervs and Arthur, as a joke, went to a fortuneteller together, a palm reader on DuPont Circle in D.C., upstairs, above one of the businesses. The woman looked at each of their hands, pronounced that they would end up married to each other, and that they would have children together. As they left, ten dollars poorer, the two of them laughed, thinking that, because they went in together, the woman thought they were a couple — which they weren't. She told them what she thought they wanted to hear. Or maybe she told them exactly what they *did* want to hear.

Trust me, I've known oracles and what they do is interpret the present and turn it into a possible future. And those are the better ones. Lots of them are just cons and bullshit artists. Back to my story. The day they were married, Dervs, eight years a vegetarian, ate a plateful of bacon at a Denny's breakfast buffet in Harrisburg, Pennsylvania. She relished every salty, greasy chew of that bacon, food she hadn't eaten in years, food that was forbidden, chancy, different. That's what Arthur was for her — the good boy, the one who brought joy instead of tears to a relationship, the one she relished for not giving her much to fight about, even though he was a meat-eater.

The day they were married, neither of them was thinking about negative possibilities, about the worse of *for better and. . . .* They got married with Arthur saying, "We'll die together. That way neither of us has to live without the other." That's as far as they got with the worse part.

The neuropsychologist who tested Dervs following her own brain injury — short-lived though it was — told her that she performed in the ninetieth percentiles in all the tests except the spatial ones, in which she performed in the seventieth and eightieth percentiles. He told her what she could do to overcome this deficit was to wrap space in words. For instance, if she wanted to remember where on Main Street the paint store was, she should tell herself it was the building with the yellow awning next to one with a red-brick facade. She learned to wrap in words without much trouble, and soon it seemed to her that her spatial sense had improved, although she could never be sure if it was her senses improving or whether her words clicked in automatically when she was trying to locate something.

The neuropsychologist, who had his daughter's photograph as his computer wallpaper — Dervs liked that — also told her a brain injury as long and extensive as Arthur's meant he had very little cognitive cushion left. What that translated to was that when his body was under attack physically — from a surgery, healing from the fixator removal — he could lose some cognitive function.

Arthur was also suffering from emotional lability — frequent mood changes and unpredictable episodes of emotional displays. In Arthur's case, anger seemed to be the predominant new emotion. Fast and furious the displays would come, without warning, with little or no provocation. Dervs liked another term for this better. She liked the term "emotional incontinence." Apparently this is Head Injury 101, and her study was just beginning. According to Arthur's former therapist, most marriages don't survive head injury because it is difficult for partners to figure out what is head injury and what is just not working.

This was not Dervs's problem. She knew what parts of Arthur's new behavior were brain injury. She just didn't like them.

She wanted to go to Delphi to the great oracle of Apollo to get a new reading. She wanted to go back in time — could oracles do that? — and have a reversal of future, the new one without a car crash. She would offer many delicacies to Apollo for that one small favor.

But when she researched the oracle, she found that Delphi was located on the southwest spur of Mount Parnassus in Greece, and that there was a fissure on the side of the mountain from which gas was emitted. This was gas from the earth's heart and

it gave the neighborhood goats seizures. The goat-
herds themselves were given to convulsions and wild
ravings. The locals called these ravings "divine rev-
elations," and when that got around, the priests of
Apollo were all over it, and moved in to take advantage of the gaseous outpourings. For Dervs, this was a
bit like finding rat droppings on the carpet.

Yesterday was five months since the accident. I look back and consider how naïve I was — I originally thought that it would take us about six months to recover from this, and at five, we are just beginning. But there is good news. Yesterday, Arthur took a shower, with Sallie's help, and then dressed himself and took his pills on his own. He met with Liz, who told him he would be walking with just one crutch by next week. And here is the big news: I went out for dinner with Cherise and Ann last night and Arthur got Wally to bed.

Wally gave himself a bath before I left at 7:30 p.m., and then he and Arthur read together, after which Wally spent half an hour giving Arthur a demonstration of BMX tricks — minus the bicycle — and lessons in terminology before he was ready to sleep. He said to Arthur, "I miss Mom. I wish she was here."

"But I'm here."

"I still miss Mom. Tell her to come in and kiss me."

Arthur told me this because it upset him. He wants to be enough for Wally when he is the parent on duty. But Wally isn't used to him being enough anymore. He is used to seeing his father incapacitated. Nevertheless, it does feel good to be able to go out and leave Arthur in charge, if only for a couple hours.

Even before the accident, I spent more time with Wally than Arthur did. I continued teaching and writing after Wally was born, although it became clear that I didn't have time to do everything, and spending time with Wally was my priority. I stopped teaching when he was about eighteen months old. Among my happiest memories are walking with Wally to and from preschool. We lived in D.C. in a neighborhood called Cleveland Park, and it turned out there was a terrific preschool there, NCRC, which had one of the best playgrounds I could imagine. Wally started going when he was three, for half days, and I loved the walks together, his small hand in mine, stopping to watch everything. Some spring days it took us 45 minutes to walk the five blocks home. We examined all bugs, many flowers, climbed the hill at Rosedale, swam in the fragrance of the days. I particularly liked early winter twilight, when the lights started flashing on inside houses. We made up stories about who lived in which houses, jumped in leaf piles, sat on the front steps when we got home and welcomed our neighbors Gordon and Martha. Time was the most important thing Wally and I shared.

These days I have been walking four to five miles a day, with friends or alone with Vinnie. This is my getting away, walking up the hill to the East Bay Regional Park trails to the thousands of acres where I can get lost, be off duty. But it too is not enough. I am always afraid nobody is home inside me; I'm afraid of collapsing in on myself with only a black hole inside sucking out life with the force of gravity. I see myself populated with sea worms, grayish mouths at both ends. The worms turn themselves inside out.

I look at a copy of a painting in *Raw Vision* magazine that draws me into it. A girl is playing a pipe organ in front of a large turquoise house. Another girl is waving from the side of the house. The turquoise house feels like the past, and the girl playing the organ used to live there, but now she is trying to make music in order to conjure herself back to the time when she was waving in the yard, waving and dancing.

Arthur is walking with one crutch and one eye patch and trying to track his life with mine these days because we've been dealing with this ovarian cyst the docs in Oregon found. Dr. Yuan wanted me to get a sonogram, so we could determine if the cyst had grown since it was measured on the CT scan at St. Charles.

Two weeks ago, I did that. Here's the thing about these medical tests: You have to go through them alone. You are lying on a table and someone is moving an apparatus over you or you are alone in a body-length tube. You are on your own, and the rooms are always cold.

My cold and lonely sonogram showed a couple of "worrisome" factors, according to Dr. Yuan. First, the cyst has grown and, second, it has become vascular. I didn't ask her what that meant, although I believe it must mean that the cyst has taken on a life of its own, has figured a way to hook into my body and feed on it rather than float free. Apparently even cysts don't like being alone. So mine has this new life, and Dr. Yuan says it should come out, just to be sure. She says most of these cysts are benign, and that I don't have blood in mine, so that is a good sign. How can it be vascular without blood? She also says the CA 125 test, which is a cancer tumor marker, came in at 11, a low number. Concern starts at 35, so I am well under that.

My surgery was scheduled for the eighteenth, five days from now. Dr. Yuan wanted to coordinate it with an oncological surgeon, Jeffrey Stern, in case there is a problem. But I just got a call saying the surgeon's schedule changed and now my surgery is on Thursday, March 27. That's seven months to the day from the accident. The change in time of the surgery made Arthur angry. He had already lined up our friend Anne Bloom (lots of Annes in the story, aren't there?), who is a law professor, to come stay with us for a week during her spring break. His parents are scheduled to come for the week after that. Now he has to reschedule, so Anne will be here for a long weekend following the surgery; the parents come after that. I am not feeling good about any of this.

Anne Bloom just left and we have a couple of days until Arthur's parents get here. Anne's visit was wonderful not just because she is beautiful and entertaining and she cooked wonderful meals, but also because she took Arthur out to play. They went shopping and, in addition to books and CDs, Arthur bought a cane. He came home walking on it, or trying. He has to learn to walk with it, to balance this new body with new parts. Cherise is back from a semester's fellowship at Harvard and has offered to take care of Wally while I am in the hospital. My friend Ann Cummins and Rikki will wait out the surgery with Arthur. We have become efficient medical event organizers. We know when to have people on duty, and we are fortunate enough to have them.

Meanwhile, I feel as if there is bad sorcery at work in the universe and our planet is catching the shock waves. Last week, Laura Rothenberg died. She was a twenty-two-year-old woman with cystic fibrosis who was doing Radio Diaries about her life. She had been a student at Brown University, left because of complications from her CF, and had a lung transplant that her body ultimately rejected. I told everyone to listen to this young woman talking about her life. The world is poorer without her; for me she was more important than most politicians and world leaders because, even though she had a fatal disease, she wasn't compromised by it. Her diaries felt real and as truthful as she could make them. I believe this not just because my son has CF, but as any parent who wishes the world were better than it is.

Another hospital with bad interior color. This time the pale beige and green with splashes of mustard remind me of rotting corpses, which you would think of as brown, not beige, right? I hate sitting here, waiting to be taken to the surgi-center, everyone smiling and polite while I want to be screaming. No one here is screaming. Why not? When did we get so damned polite? When did we lose our animality, our ability to show ourselves in public, our fear of examining our asses, licking our wounds?

Here I am, another damned polite patient, waiting quietly to be knocked out and cut up. When they call me, Arthur and I obediently follow an attendant down to the surgery center in the basement. Arthur sits in the waiting room while I am taken to a dressing room, told to put my clothes in a plastic bag with my name on it, and given two gowns to put on, the bottom one to open in the front, the top one to open in the back, and a pair of socks. Then I am weighed and led to a bed, where I am covered with warm blankets and a warmer filled with hot air, so I can be comfortable while I wait.

When Arthur gets to my bed, I am toasty and cozy and trying to be calm. I am focusing on the woman in a bed across the walkway who, when I saw her in the waiting area upstairs, was dressed in jeans and a sweater, looked in charge of herself. Now I hear her speaking in a squeaky, terrified voice. While I complain about none of us crying out, I am unnerved by her sense of terror — or what I interpret as her sense of terror. Maybe the terror is mine.

I have to be wheeled, in the bed, into an elevator that goes up to the operating rooms. The anesthesiologist talks to me about giving me a little something in my IV to keep me calm. In the operating room, cold again, I am transferred from the bed to the operating table, and that is all I remember.

I wake up in the recovery room, where, really, all I can call up is a white fog. The nurses tell me I have to stay overnight; the operation was too involved to let me go home tonight. I am disappointed and think maybe something went wrong, but I can't make my thoughts go further than that.

The next thing I know is that I am in a bed in a double room. Mine is the bed nearer the door and the bathroom. Arthur and Ann and Rikki are here, and Arthur is smiling as I open my eyes.

"It's okay," he says. "There was no cancer."

"Really?" I mumble. "Are you sure?"

"That's what the doctor told us. You're home free."

I feel as if circus performers are juggling, clowning, trapezing in my head, and they are happy. Ann hands me copies of *Vogue* and *Elle* magazines. She says she picked them up for my reading pleasure, that one gets to read anything while in the hospital. As we are all celebrating the good news, Dr. Yuan comes in, thin and smiling, and tells me everything looked good, that she and the other doctors saw no evidence of cancer; there was no need to call on Dr. Stern.

*Jeez, and we changed the schedule for him.*

She also tells me that she did drop the cyst as she was removing it and it burst, but that she irrigated the site well, so that didn't present a problem. She does want me to stay in the hospital another day. She says if anything changes, she'll come by tomorrow, but she's sure it will all be fine.

Finally, we catch a break. It feels as if a color wash of relief has swept over us.

Turns out I have to stay here until tomorrow morning, so I've been hanging out, reading the magazines Ann brought me. There was another woman in this room last night, in the bed over by the window, but she left this morning and we didn't really speak. She had friends visit last night and they talked about how her hair was going to grow out soon, so I guess she had some kind of surgery after chemotherapy treatments. All I could think was how happy I am not to have to do that. The late-afternoon light is coming in, casting everything with a filmy haze. Arthur said he would come by later this evening.

I look up and see Dr. Yuan walking toward me. I smile at her, and she returns the gesture with a pale upturn of her mouth.

"Listen," she says, "I have some bad news for you. The pathology on your cyst shows some cancer cells."

*This cannot be happening. Did I just enter some Twilight Zone? I can't even grasp this.*

"Are you sure?" I say.

"Yes, I just came back from the lab. I couldn't believe it, so I went to the lab to check. It's true. And I also have to tell you that because the cyst ruptured, it is automatically stage three cancer. The good news is that I took both ovaries out, and while the right one had cancer cells, there was no cancer in the left one. And if the cancer had spread it would have gone first to the other ovary."

*What the fuck is stage three?*

"What does that mean? What do I have to do?" I ask.

"I want you to see Dr. Stern, the surgeon who was on call. My office will make an appointment for you. You will probably have to have chemo treatments, but you can discuss that with him. He's the best there is, so you will be in good hands."

"Can you please call my husband and tell him what you told me?" I ask.

"Yes, I'll call him a little later tonight. I am very sorry about this," she says. "There were two other doctors in the operating room and we each thought everything looked fine."

"Okay," I say. "Just please call Arthur for me. Thanks."

"I will talk to you later," she says, and leaves.

I don't even know what to do with this information. I am exhausted by it and frozen. I go to sleep.

I wake to the insistent ringing of the bedside phone. I want it to shut up, but move myself around to answer it. I know it is Arthur, but I don't want to talk to him, or anyone, about this.

He has spoken with Dr. Yuan and knows about the lab results.

"I am so sorry, Honey," he tells me. "We're going to get through this. I can't believe it."

"Yeah, me either," I say. "Did she tell you it's stage three? That's what she told me. What does that mean?"

"Well, it turns out it's not, according to her. She said she did some research, and even though the cyst ruptured, it's still stage one or two, early. The important thing is, we will get through it, whatever it takes. Can you hold onto that?"

"I don't know what I can hold onto," I tell him. "It's all too much for me to even absorb. I want to go to sleep and have it be some other world when I wake up."

## SEE SPOT RUN

England, Wales, New England—legends of a black dog run through the countrysides. In the British Isles, the dog has fiery eyes. In a Connecticut story, the first time you see the black dog it is good luck, the second time bad luck, the third time death. Multiple colors of black dog t-shirts from the tavern of the same name in Martha's Vineyard populate East Coast streets all summer. In the novel *Treasure Island*, the pirate Black Dog is a harbinger of coming violence, "a pale, tallowy creature, wanting two fingers of the left hand. . . ."

This herald of trouble, this is the black dog Dervs has walked with since her mother's death. Dervs's black dog is a companion named cancer. Minutes after her mother's death from breast cancer at age fifty, the resident physician on duty at St. Luke's Hospital in Bethlehem, Pennsylvania, told Dervs that she would most likely inherit her mother's disease, and she might want to start getting mammograms early. In her heart, Dervs believed her mother's death was a suicide—suicide by cancer.

Here is what happened: Dervs's mother had a benign cyst removed from her right breast when her daughter was a sophomore in college. That was the last Dervs knew about it until shortly after she graduated. Her mother came home from a job-related physical one day in June and said she had to go into the hospital the next day. The story Dervs got from her mother was that several months after having the original cyst removed, the site of the incision started to become discolored and lumpy, so her mother went back to her doctor, who told her it was scar tissue. Dervs's mother then proceeded to ignore, for the next two and a half years, the growing lump and discoloration, and her doctor died as well, so she said she had no one to contact about the growing mass. That ended with this physical. She said the physician told her: "Tomorrow. Hospital. I'll contact a surgeon."

The next day, Dervs's mother entered the hospital; later that week she joined the secret cadre of women with mastectomies. The lymph nodes removed during the surgery all came back positive for cancer. In the space of a year, she underwent radiation therapy, had her ovaries removed, even went back to work for a couple months, and then returned to the hospital to die. That was the year Dervs lived in Russia. She came home twice to see her mother.

The first time was after her mother called her in Moscow to tell Dervs that her father was unwilling to face his wife's impending death. There was the will, the cemetery, too many things to mention to deal with, and she didn't know how she was going to do it alone. Even though Dervs knew this was manipulation, she borrowed five hundred dollars from her boyfriend, took two weeks off from her job, and flew to Bethlehem in April to help her mother prepare for death. They went to the lawyer's, the bank, the cemetery to purchase a family plot, the funeral home, where they met with Dino the mortician. Dervs's mother chose the clothes and jewelry she wanted to be buried in and gave Dervs complete instructions for the funeral, down to the note that she did not want anyone to place flowers on the casket. She chose psalms and hymns for the funeral service at the church. She tried to control her death, to make sure the spiders inside her mind didn't escape and make things messy. Dervs went along with it and then went back to Russia.

Two months later, Dervs received news that her mother had been hospitalized and would probably die before Dervs could get home. That was Dervs's intent. She wanted to return to a dead woman, so she put off leaving for a couple of days, citing complications packing up and getting the appropriate visas. In spite of Dervs's best efforts, her mother was still alive when Dervs arrived home, and she spent the next two weeks in her mother's hospital room, sleeping on a chair because her mother didn't want to be alone. Her father had already used all the time he was allowed off from his job, and her mother refused to allow anyone else, even her own siblings, to see her. On a Saturday morning, while Dervs was at home taking a shower and her father was at the hospital, her mother died, and the doctor told Dervs about the black dog that would, from now on, accompany her.

For Dervs, the most poignant moment surrounding her mother's death was when she and Dino, the mortician, and Dervs's Aunt Martha closed and locked the coffin. Her mother had asked that Dervs be there when the coffin was closed, so she was. Dino was good enough to provide straight scotch for Dervs and her aunt, and then it was a simple job to shut the lid and watch her mother go into darkness. Just the way she had wanted.

We are driving in Ann's blue RAV4, going to pick up
Wally from school. Since neither Arthur nor I can drive
right now — I have to wait two weeks post-surgery — our
friends have been chauffeuring us. Cherise or Geoff picks
up Wally in the morning, and Ann brings him home after
school. This is Ann's first new car; she bought it after
she sold *Red Ant House*, her book of short stories. The
first time I met Ann, in 1986, in graduate school at Johns
Hopkins University, she had just driven from New Mexico
to Baltimore in a 1971 burgundy Ford Fairlane. That was
one big car with one big grill, a long, thin drink-of-water
car. You could really spread out in that car. She bought
it from an older man in Bloomfield, New Mexico, who
had stored it in his barn when he stopped driving. Ann
says she knew a good deal when she saw it. Even though
the car needed tires and some engine work and several
families of mice had taken up residence, it had only been
driven for ten thousand miles. That car was ready for a
cross-country trip.

Ann and I got to know each other standing in
line — either at the housing office or the post office on
campus. She was wearing old jeans and cowboy boots,
and I wanted to meet her just for her style. I had seen
her around; we were both in the graduate writing program, but she was in fiction and I was in poetry. Word
was she had already published some short stories. I got
in line behind her and we started talking. She was taking

off to New York City for the weekend, and then told me she was nervous because she'd been having a fling with a guy who turned out to be a junkie and now she needed to get an HIV test. And there I was worried because I sat in my poetry seminars and didn't have a clue about the terminology. What was I going to say to her: I'm nervous because I don't know the difference between a ghazal and a caesura? I need to get a poetry test. Ann told me later that she had wanted to get to know me because I spoke with authority and seemed to get things done. I think, in the end, what we recognized in each other was our working class backgrounds. My father worked in a steel mill, hers in a uranium mining operation. And we were there in line together at a fancy university. Who would have thought?

Seventeen years later, we are driving together in this fancy blue car, heading south on Highway 13 toward Mills College, and she asks me how I am feeling.

"I feel like I need to get well, get through this cancer because it's important for Wally and Arthur. Wally is eight and Arthur is an invalid. But how am I feeling? I feel tired; right now I don't care if I live or die. I feel as if death would be an escape from this never-ending string of trauma."

Ann grabs my shoulder hard with her right hand and shakes it.

"Here's what I want that therapist of yours to tell you. I want her to tell you that you should want to live for yourself, not for Arthur and Wally, for yourself."

I start to cry. My friend is stretching across our

histories and has figured out what I need — something I didn't realize until now — which is to not be alone. For me, the center of the cancer diagnosis was utter solitude, as if I were alone inside a black balloon floating somewhere outside the earth. The struggle with cancer is the struggle to keep company, to not be sucked out into space by yourself, without companionship.

I remember my joyless mother's death, her last two weeks in the hospital when she was pumped full of morphine. She had dreams about being a child and seeing puppies. She spoke in a child's voice about how cute they were. When she was more cognizant, she told me how her life had been good and what a good man my father was, how he had made her happy. She said how close she felt to God. Revisionist history. Her life was a misery; she and my father hadn't been happy together in my lifetime; she didn't believe in God, at least not in any way I had ever heard of. But that was my mother's death, and her death will not be mine.

Arthur and I have been fighting. He had lined up a string of people to come help us even though I told him after Al and Marcia left that I was okay without help. My incision had healed well, and I could do anything but heavy lifting for another couple weeks. But he insisted we needed more help, and he asked his older sister Robin to come here from Pennsylvania for a week.

"What if you fall or faint? I won't be able to help you," said Arthur.

I was staring at the stainless steel pots hanging on the kitchen wall. Thinking at the same time how I had rarely used the double boiler, I said, "And what are the chances of that? You can use the phone to get somebody here to help me. I need some time and space without anybody else in the house."

"What about going to doctor's appointments. I can't drive you."

"I can drive me. Who do you think has been driving you and Wally and me everywhere? And if I can't do it, Ann or Amy or Cherise will. I have that covered."

"But you're the one who needs help now. You shouldn't need to have it covered. You should be taking care of yourself, getting sleep, taking naps."

"What I need is my house to myself. We already have the occupational and physical therapists coming in. Somebody comes every day. And you need that. I need to at least have nights alone, not having to entertain or worry about what someone else needs or is doing," I said.

"You won't have to. I can take care of Robin," said Arthur.

"Why not just take care of me?" I said, with great indignation, and walked out of the kitchen.

But Arthur couldn't hear me, and Robin flew out here, which we paid for, and four days later I told him, hysterically, that she had to go home. He and I were sitting in bed and in the loudest whisper I could manage, so Robin wouldn't hear me, I said, "She has to go! I am losing my mind. I just can't have another person here, no matter how nice she is."

Normally, I wouldn't have done that. I would have figured *what's a couple of days?* But I am not normal now, right down to thinking, *I'm the one with cancer. Why don't I get to decide what I need?*

"Okay," said Arthur, "I'll talk to her tomorrow. I don't know what I'm going to tell her."

"Whatever you tell her, I'm going to end up the bad guy. You set me up for this by not listening to me, and now your sister is going to think I don't like her. Just tell her the truth. It's not about her."

"She's not going to see it that way."

"You know what? That's not my problem," I said, and pulled the covers up and pillows down to build a sleeping shelter.

Before the inferno, we went, the three of us, to my appointment with Jeffrey Stern, way the heck and gone in San Pablo at a medical center near a casino. I am going to have to get used to filling out pages of forms, writing that I have cancer, recalling every medical procedure I've ever had, waiting in rooms filled with desperate people. The meeting with Dr. Stern wasn't terrible. He told me the prognosis was good for getting rid of this puppy, and he gave me the name of the oncologist he wants me to see for chemotherapy — Martha Tracy. Her office is in Berkeley, much closer to home. Stern said that after the chemo he would go in to do a clean-up operation, check for any remaining cancer cells, remove unnecessary body parts. I didn't ask too many questions because I don't want to know things like what my unnecessary body parts are.

After all this, I count on Charlotte to paste me back together once again. I talk to her about having post traumatic stress disorder, PTSD, and she says, "Honey, there is no post about it. You are still in the middle of trauma."

"I don't care about what the hell I'm in the middle of," I say. Right now, what I feel mostly is how much I hate Arthur for creating this situation with Robin, which I end up having to deal with. He must hate me too because he was just trying to get what *he* needed. But at this moment, I really don't care what he needs.

"You have to imagine that he is a person who grew up having his needs met, that his parents taught him it was all right to have needs. You lived in a very different place, where it wasn't okay for you to have needs, where your mother took up all the space with her needs and behavior. Arthur isn't trying to hurt you with his needs. You torture yourself when you want anything, for having any desires.

We have to work on that."

This all sounds like a big bunch of gobbledygook to me. I just want to stop feeling the way I do.

I leave Charlotte's office and, as I walk to the parking lot, think that at least the news on the driving front is good. Arthur is scheduled to have his first driving lesson on the eighteenth. He has to take lessons because he is a one-eyed guy now. His left eye is still swollen shut from the fistula repair, and no one can tell if it will ever work in concert with the right eye. He continues to wear an eye patch, has even found a website that sells funky ones. I expressed the opinion that black was better than one with musical notes or stars or ducks if he wanted people to take him seriously. Thing is, I don't know what he wants. We are both falling apart.

A month ago, Wally had another CF appointment that didn't go well. Dr. McQuitty wanted to put him in the hospital because he was having a flare-up. This time we were told there was a ten- to twenty-percent chance we could change the course of the flare at home. When Dr. McQuitty said this to us, Arthur's face, patch and all, started to drip off his head. I'd never seen a face dissolve before; it was as if all the muscles slackened and fell and dripped into his shirt collar.

"We'll try it at home first," I said.

And here we are now, the three of us, waiting to find out the results of Wally's pulmonary function tests and whether Dr. Lewis (McQuitty's partner) hears the flare's telltale crackles and wheezes in Wally's lungs. Wally's been working hard on his respiratory therapy, inhaling a series of drugs designed to attack the bacterial colonies that have taken up residence in his lungs. Dr. McQuitty said it is no surprise that Wally is having more flare-ups than usual because of the stress the accident and its aftermath have caused.

Today, Dr. Lewis says the news is good for now. Although Wally's lung capacity is low — seventy-seven percent, the lungs are clear of wheezes and there are only a couple crackles in one lobe. We will continue our treatments at home and come back for another appointment in two weeks. A bullet dodged.

Ann read from *Red Ant House* last night at A Clean

Well-Lighted Place for Books in San Francisco. Arthur stayed with Wally, and I got to have a night from my former life: attending a reading and then sharing drinks and dinner with a group of friends where we talked about art and literature and lives that were not crowded with medical emergencies.

I need this air, this time away from my family, away from Arthur, who is seriously depressed and crying all the time. I told him yesterday that I couldn't absorb his terrors any more, that he needs to get more help, see a new therapist, frequently. Today he told me he thinks I am treating him dismissively.

Cherise says it is unnerving to see Arthur behave as if he has no power or authority and then have outbursts to regain some control. Nothing in his life has prepared him for this. The brain injury has left him a person who has trouble even making decisions — *so* not his former style. I've asked the doctors about the time frame for recovery from his kind of injury, and the answers are always fuzzy: most improvement comes in the first year, but some aspects of recovery take as long as five years to manifest, and some never comes.

I still feel heightened anxiety and uncertainty from my own head injury. Last night when I got home, Wally was lying in bed coughing and couldn't stop. Arthur was asleep; he has been taking Ambien so he can sleep through the muscle and bone pain he feels at night. I suppose that is his body healing. After nothing else worked to quiet Wally's cough, I gave him a teaspoon of cough syrup with codeine, which quickly calmed his cough and put him to sleep. Then I spent the whole night awake, skulking in and out of his room, imagining I had poisoned him because the codeine could interact with his CF medicines. I got up every hour to make sure he was breathing. I read through the literature accompanying his medications looking for possible problems. What kind of mother am I?

Perhaps *my* being poisoned is just comeuppance. This is my first trip to the Cancer Center, and I think the best thing about it must be the valet parking. You drive up and one of the efficient, red-jacketed attendants gives you a ticket and whisks your car away. I think of this as luxury until I look around and see people getting out of cars and into wheelchairs and frail men and women driven and accompanied into the center by relatives or friends.

Arthur has come with me for this visit, walking through the double doors with his cane. I am struck by how large and crowded the center is. The reception area is on the right where two or three assistants, depending on the moment, take your name and give you a buzzer that convulses when it is your turn. The wall on the left is entirely windows and glass doors. You try to find a seat in one of three U-shaped seating areas opposite the windows. These are each comprised of stuffed chairs surrounding a center table laid out with magazines and a large vase of flowers. Nearly all the chairs are filled, a lot of chairs, a lot of people.

Cell phones don't work here, but someone behind me is plugged into Avril Lavigne. At first I can't tell who the patients are; most of the people are in pairs, and then I start to notice women wearing head scarves, some wearing wigs. There is, also, apparently a cancer cough. I hear it from several people, kind of a small cough, lightly phlegmy. Maybe it's a chemo cough. I don't know. Young people, old people, men, women, and a couple people I can't tell their sex. There is a person across the way — sixties, short, curly gray hair, wearing jeans and an olive-green sweater, black socks and loafers. This person, whose sex I can't determine, is drinking coffee, reading a book. One of the nurses comes up after a while and addresses him as Irwin, so I know. The Cancer Center holds mysteries.

It takes twenty minutes before I get my blood drawn. This bloodletting is apparently standard procedure before doctor visits and chemotherapy treatments. They tell me it will take about thirty minutes to get the results from the blood tests. We wait about forty-five minutes before I get called to see the doctor. Her assistant takes my blood pressure, temperature, and asks me to get on a scale to be weighed. After that, I am shown to an exam room. I run back into the reception area and retrieve Arthur to go with me.

After about fifteen minutes, a woman walks in with a smile.

"You're one of the lucky ones," she says. "I'm Dr. Tracy."

"I am?"

"You are. It's not often that ovarian gets caught this early. There aren't usually symptoms. You just happened to have been in a situation where you had a CT scan and the cyst showed up. I'm being selfish here. I like having the lucky ones."

She tells me she is recommending two chemo drugs: carboplatin and taxol in six treatments, three weeks apart.

I will lose my hair and my energy, will be susceptible to infections, will likely be nauseous and exhausted, and I will have to spend a lot of time at the Cancer Center being treated and looked after. My treatments will begin on May 7 and, if all goes well, end on August 20. Maybe it's me, but I don't feel that lucky.

Events are flurrying through the air. We just learned from Jeff Foote that we will get a little money from the uninsured motorist fund, through our own insurance. That should help with medical bills for a while, although it will be a lot less than we would have gotten if Mr. Adney had actually *had* insurance. Some things we can't change.

Arthur has a new therapist, whom he saw for the first time last week. This should give us both some relief. I don't have enough internal sponge to absorb his difficulties as well as my own.

But the big news for Arthur is that today he is having his final driving lesson, eight months after the accident, and he will be able to maneuver a car. This is such a bonus for us, and comes at the right time, when I may have trouble driving on some days as a result of the chemo. Now the challenge is to get Arthur up to speed on Wally's schedule. This is Oakland; there are no school buses. I drive the little bugger to and from school every day and to his other appointments.

And the little bugger still has a cough, so I am worried once again that he may have to be hospitalized. I don't know how we could handle that. I wouldn't be able to stay with him because of my chemo, and I don't know how Arthur could manage. He still has people coming in a couple times a week to help him with physical needs, although he is working as hard as he can to be functional without help. His whole world must feel topsy-turvy. He can't really stand up straight because his legs are different lengths, so his spine is crooked. His left eye is still not tracking with the right, so he is still "patched up," which gives him a different view of the world in a variety of ways. I feel as if we belong in a Charles Dickens novel, one of those pathetic families in rags, begging on the streets: the crippled father, tubercular and coughing child, wasted mother.

Arthur, in spite of his new view of the world, is trying to do more work, get up to speed on his law firm. His board of directors just met in Seattle, and although he couldn't go in person, they conferenced him in to participate. This is step one in his feeling as if he is a member of society again, as if he can begin the process of getting back to his old job. Before the accident, Arthur was the guy who could juggle ten things and make sure each of them got to the desired result. He was good at dealing with other lawyers, supervising communications and development departments, helping to write and edit Supreme Court briefs, and come up with strategies for winning cases — always on the side of the underdog. This is a man who knew his mission early, when he was a teenager.

I used to say to him, "How could you know at age fourteen that you wanted to become a public interest lawyer? Nobody even knows what that is at fourteen. There are some odd ducks operating in your brain."

Now I hope all those odd ducks wake up and get back to work.

Arthur's also been getting out a little bit with friends.

He and Curtis went for dinner the other night, and he came home and thanked me for having pushed it. Our friends are amazing. Recently Ann has been schlepping all of us to appointments, ferrying Wally around, helping Arthur. The same with Amy and Cherise. We never expect our friendships or our marriages to be tested in such extreme ways, and when they are, if we are really fortunate, they turn out to be more valuable than we could have imagined. Your friends can save you.

After Wally was born, my friend Molly — whose daughter is a year older than Wally — told me one of the amazing aspects of having a baby was the amount of gear it involved, gear for riding in the car, gear for going to a restaurant, gear for going to a friend's or relative's home, gear for every occasion. Nothing is simple. That's how this expedition into chemo-land feels. There are classes in preparation, special stores that sell wigs and head paraphernalia, nutritionists to see. All this is in addition to doctors' appointments and the chemo itself.

This afternoon I spend from two to four thirty in chemo class with a thirty-five-ish nurse named Jennifer leading the discussion. Jennifer has gorgeous, long, reddish-blonde hair. This is a tough thing to see for a group of people about to lose theirs. In the class, there are a number of women from about forty to sixty years old, of varying ethnicities, some with partners, others, like me, alone. There is an older woman and her daughter, and another woman, maybe in her late twenties or early thirties. There is an older couple in their later seventies. He is getting both chemo and radiation.

We are all friendly and try not to appear panicked as we talk about mouth sores and special toothpastes and mouthwashes, port-o-catheters, keeping away from people who have colds or are ill, gardening with gloves on because of germs in the soil, taking medicine for leg pain and nausea, insomnia, wearing hats and sunscreen

because the chemo drugs make you more susceptible to sunburn. One of the women who looks pulled
together — polo shirt, khakis, loafers — there with her
husband, says the name of the game at her house is
*Survivor*. I don't get the joke at first, and then I realize she
is referring to the TV series.

After an hour, all I can think is *get me out of here.
How rude will it be to walk out?*

Today is my first chemo treatment. As a gift to ourselves, Arthur and I went out for dinner together last night to Café Rouge, a little restaurant on Fourth Street in Berkeley. I forgot that it is spring and was delighted by ordering a fava bean salad — *Who can even say "fava bean" without thinking of Hannibal Lecter?* — and Meyer lemon risotto with spring peas, English peas, and scallops. Arthur had steak frites. And wine, I had wine. This is my tiny window for wine between the time I had to lay off alcohol because of my head injury and the start of chemo. Definitely two glasses of wine. Arthur doesn't drink anyway, so his warning not to have alcohol for a year doesn't affect him in any way.

Being in a restaurant with white tablecloths and attentive waiters was like being in a cocoon for an evening. We have so little time for our relationship, our marriage; just staying afloat nowadays takes all our energy. This was Arthur's moment to tell me he is committed to getting back, to overcoming his physical and emotional challenges so he can be *the guy* again, so he can feel like he is doing his job well, so he can help take care of his family. And it was my moment to say that I need him to do that — I'm tired and worn out and heading into a disaster zone that I can't anticipate. We are both encouraged by Wally's latest news; again we have skirted a possible CF hospitalization.

Yesterday I also had my port-o-catheter installed —

sounds like an automotive part. A port, which looks like a bottle cap just under the skin, is connected to an artery, and allows you to get chemotherapy without having to start a new IV each time. A nurse pokes a needle into the port and you're good to go. The installation was fine. It takes a little time in Interventional Radiology, where they use screens to guide the insertion. I was awake for the procedure, in a kind of twilight state. Arthur was waiting for me when I was finished, and he drove me home.

Ann picks me up at 8:30 this morning and takes me to the Cancer Center. The treatment area is a lot less airy and friendly than the waiting room. (The staff refers to it as "the Cave.") Here there are no windows and the lights are fluorescent in the ceiling. The treatment rooms radiate around the outside of the area. The center of the interior room consists of a long desk that is the medical hub where records are kept, scheduling is done, and nurses and docs pick up information and medicines. Each patient has a nurse who administers the drugs.

The treatment rooms themselves accommodate two patients. Each of us gets a cushy chair with leg rests that groan up and backs that groan down. While I am getting set up in my chair, Ann and I talk about books and writers and throw in a little gossip to keeps things spicy. My nurse, Lisa, starts giving me drugs through my port and then sits with me for the first fifteen minutes of the taxol drip to make sure I don't have any adverse reactions to it. Taxol is administered very slowly; it takes two hours, then I will change to the carboplatin. This is a busy day for me.

I am visited by Gale, the social worker, and Bernadette, the dietician, another nurse named Kathie, and my doctor, Martha Tracy. As Dr. Tracy is leaving, she says, "You are going to do fine through this, and it will be over before you know it."

I want to kiss her.

Ann takes notes whenever it seems appropriate, mostly during the dietician's talk. Here is an excerpt:

— *Non-citrus, cold foods, yogurt if tolerated*
— *Glutamine to counteract achiness (or*
  *L-glutamine)*
— *Lots of fluid first couple of days (8 ounces, 8 x*
  *day)*
— *Salty things (here Ann draws a picture of Mr.*
  *Peanut)*
— *Dry food to settle upset stomach*

The chemo is over in about three hours, and Ann takes me home. I feel okay, mostly sludge around, moving from sofa to chair to bed, where I sleep fitfully through the night.

The one thing I have to deal with is what to do about my head, not what's in it, what's on it. I'm going to lose my hair, so I have to decide what I want to do. Arthur's response is "commando" — no underwear, no head covering.

"Why don't you just macho it?" he asks.

"Maybe I will, but right now. I'm not ready," I say. "I'm going to ask Wally what he thinks."

After I explain to Wally what's going to happen and that my choices are to be bald and not worry about it, to wear hats and scarves, or to get a wig, he says, " I think I would feel better if you wore a wig."

So I make my way to a store called A Lady's Touch — the name makes me a little squirmy — and buy a wig and two scarves and a summer hat. This process takes a couple hours, and while I am there a number of other women come in. I spend some time talking to the owner, about what to expect from the chemo treatment. She is a breast cancer survivor and started the business because there was no place to go for hats and wigs over fifteen years ago, when she was having chemo and lost her own hair. After I finish talking to her and am looking at tropical headbands that attach to falls, hair floating out from them, a woman comes up to me and says, "I'm the person you want to meet."

*I do?*

Before I can say anything, she tells me that she heard

me talking to the storeowner about just getting into this process.

"Let me tell you about myself," the woman says, and before I can agree or urge her to continue, she says, "All I ever wanted from my life was to get married and have children. I didn't care about a career — for me raising children was going to be my career. I met a great man, we got married, and within the year I was diagnosed with breast cancer. The results of the treatment included that I couldn't get pregnant. I was devastated; I had no idea what I was going to do with my life, and then, through our church, we found a baby boy and adopted him. That was seventeen years ago, and today he is a musician, he's in a rock band, and he's the joy of my life."

I'm looking at this woman, still wondering why she is telling me all this. She is shorter than I am, maybe five feet two, although I'm never good at estimating height. She has thin, strawberry-colored hair and a laser look in her eyes as she speaks to me.

"I've had cancer in my lungs, my bones, even my brain," she says, "and every time I think 'just let me get through the treatment and stay alive long enough to have them come up with a new treatment for the next one.' I need to stay alive to see my son grow up."

I am unnerved by her story. I choose to believe that this woman's motive for telling me what she did is good, that she wants to give me hope, but I leave the store feeling uneasy, untethered, slimed. Here I am going into treatment believing I'll be done in six months, and there is someone telling me that the cancer doesn't stop, it just keeps invading, each time aiming for a different organ. I leave thinking that I never want to talk to another cancer patient again. They are way too freaky.

I stop on the way home to buy evening primrose oil, which the storeowner said worked for her to stop hot flashes. One of the side effects of chemo is that it smacks your body with hot flashes; I think it might smack your body into menopause, but I'm not sure. I just know the hot flashes happen, and I want to lessen their effect. I am sure there are other side effects of the chemo as well; I just don't know about them yet.

As for my hair, I have it cut short and then very short — about half an inch long — and dyed auburn-red to match the red-with-blonde-highlights wig I bought. People tell me my short hair cut is cool, enough people so I want to keep it, but it starts to fall out in a major way on May 25. I see it in the bathtub drain and go outside to towel off what's going to come out anyway. As I'm toweling, I think maybe I can communicate, channel, hook into other people whose hair has been shaved or fallen out: saints, nuns, army recruits. I am looking for a patron saint, a wing and a prayer, but I get nothing. Maybe the message is that my hair sloughing off is a metaphor for the cancer cells falling away.

I admit that I am disturbed in a mighty way by my baldness. Physical attractiveness has never come easy for me. One time in seventh or eighth grade, this girl in my class named Linda was classifying other girls. She said, "Now Susie is beautiful, and Megan is pretty, and you, well, I guess maybe you're cute." Trust me, I know middle-aged women are not cute, but whatever "maybe cute" transforms into, I try to maintain. Early on in elementary school I was skinny, had funny teeth, sticking-out hair, and other kids made fun of me because of it. I decided then that I was going to have to get through life on my brains, not my looks, but I was never independent enough not to care at all how I appeared. So this baldness: it is taking a chunk out of my self-perception.

But this is me being macho. The truth is my empty head feels like an externalization of my interior life, the one my mother inhabits, where my father is asleep on the floor for eighteen years ignoring me. Children who are not loved by their parents, you don't want to see the insides of their heads. I am afraid mine is showing.

I wear my wig around Wally so he can get used to it, but he has some concerns. I still teach a weekly poetry class at his school and one day before the class he says to me, "Mom, what if you trip and your wig comes off?"

"I guess we'll write poems about it," I say with confidence, at the same time that I am terrified this could actually happen.

A couple weeks into my baldness, Wally comes into Arthur's and my bedroom about three in the morning after he's had a nightmare, and he finds my cue ball head, which I have thus far shielded him from. It's dark, so he is fine curling up between us, going back to sleep. But in the morning he says to me, "Your head is kind of freaking me out because you don't look like my mom. I think it would help if you did some more mom things with me during the next couple of days, so I can feel like you are the same."

I feel as if I watched pieces of *my* mother fall off her all my life, psychological pieces that increased her fears. When she started to be afraid of all bugs, not just spiders and centipedes, a piece fell away; when she thought the neighbors were talking about her having an affair because she carpooled to work with a man, a piece fell away; when she started to ask me about my sex life, a piece fell away. Now that my hair has fallen away, I worry about its psychological counterpart. And I think this must sound nuts as I write it, which worries me more.

Even though it replaces the piece of me that has fallen off, I am not that comfortable wearing my wig. I keep it on around Wally, but mostly I wear a black scarf tied at the nape of my neck, topped with a black baseball cap — something I might wear even if I had hair.

On June 9, I notice my pubic hair has started to slip away as well as my eyebrows and eyelashes. My eyebrows I draw on; the rest I can't do anything about.

Rikki arrives at 9:30 a.m. to take me to my third chemo appointment. The good news is that Dr. Tracy says my blood work looks good, everything seems to be pretty much within normal parameters. I am grateful for that, although I admit to having no idea what we're measuring and what normal parameters are. I suppose if I had more time, I would. I think many of the patients here are really on top of everything. I just can't be.

Wally's last day of school was June 4, so I've been on mom duty much of the time. Arthur is doing what he can as well as he can, but he has his own body to take care of. We are a real mess of a parental body.

Today I end up sharing a room with a woman who is knitting with copper wire. Thin, she couldn't weigh more than ninety pounds, with coppery hair, she is tiny in the chair where she is hooked up to an IV. But she is smiling. And she's happy to hear that both Rikki and I are knitters because she can explain her project to us. We learn that she is receiving treatment for cancer in her bones. She tells us she started with breast cancer that migrated inward and shows us a scan of her skeleton that she has framed. We can see the black spot. Apparently she's making some kind of art piece with these X-rays. There are four pictures of her bones, four skeletons, to a sheet. She has several sheets in addition to the one that is framed. She says when she finishes this piece, she is going to call it *Out, out black spot.*

What she is knitting with the copper wire is a sculptural base for a piece that will ultimately hold a doll and, I presume, one of the skeleton scans, although I could be making that up. She doesn't say much about the doll, but I imagine it to be tiny and delicate with blue eyes and coppery hair.

During the several hours we spend with this woman, she tells us that she has been ill since she was a child. I have trouble locating age, but to me she now looks about sixty. In addition to the cancer treatment, she is receiving kidney dialysis. Her life seems to be the process of translating her illnesses into art.

When I finish my chemo, I drive us home, although I'm beginning to feel woozy. I can't tell if it's too much poison in my system, too much time at the Cancer Center, or too many black holes in my skeleton.

In addition to occasional dizziness, the chemo has destroyed my taste buds and sense of smell. I have some nausea and once got scared because I thought I was going to pass out. I called the nurse at the Cancer Center, and she told me I was experiencing vasovagal syncope, that I should lie down and elevate my feet, and it would go away. My temperature has gone up to 99 degrees a couple times but never reached 101, which is when you have to call a nurse. And I am tired, constantly, and a little muddy, murky, muddled in my thinking sometimes. The problem is, I can't always tell when those times are.

This is day three after my latest chemo, and I have taken Anzemet, Lorazepam, and Compazine to control nausea, and Vioxx to counteract the pain in my legs. My heart goes out to my liver. Today I let Arthur take care of Wally, and I just take care of myself. The two boys are out doing errands: getting groceries, clothes for Wally, propane in the tank for the gas grill. I think Arthur is improving by leaps and bounds — okay maybe not leaps and bounds, but he is walking better every day. He, however, is frustrated that his legs aren't healing any faster. He continues to walk with a cane and still has a Trendelenburg Gait. While that sounds like an architectural monument in Berlin, it is an abnormal walk caused by weak muscles in the lower limb, the gluteus medius and gluteus minimus. Because Arthur's legs are different lengths — his left is now shorter by an inch and a half than his right — when he walks, he kind of lurches toward the left to compensate for the unevenness of his hips. Here's a guy who just wants to get back to normal and he is lurchy. The doctor has told him it will be years and several more operations until he is in a position to be able to correct the uneven leg lengths. I suppose the question becomes: What does normal look like?

A year ago, Ann, her husband Steve, Cherise and Geoff, and Arthur and Wally and I were all in Kona together for the marathon. Who would have thought that a year later I would be having cancer treatment and

Arthur would be hoping to walk steadily and get his eye patch on straight each morning. In spite of all the horror and chaos, I look out the window this morning at Vinnie, standing among the flowers at the front of the house, and am struck by the beauty of the entire picture. How does this happen, our resilience as a species?

Here is a joke from Wally: "What's the last thing that goes through a bug's head when he crashes into a window?"

Answer: "His butt."

## HEROES

Dervs doesn't want to talk about cancer treatment anymore, but there are a couple things you need to know. One of them is that, in spite of the fact that they scared her, she regarded the cancer patients she met while getting her own treatment to be heroes. These were the people who looked at their fear, lived with it every day, recognized their mortality and their fear of mortality. These were the people who, if you met them on the street and didn't know they were sick, wouldn't spend their time telling you.

Dervs looked at the other hairless women and thought cancer treatment was a lot like income taxes: it's enough that you have to pay the tax, often to support what you don't agree with, but you also have to do it on time and fill out complicated forms correctly. These patients not only had cancer and were going through treatments with side effects that ranged from nausea to weight loss to weight gain to bone pain to neuropathy, but in addition, they had to think about losing their hair and what to do about it. Insult added to injury. And it wasn't just women, there were plenty of men, a number of them young, and while it was perhaps easier for them to just cover baldness with a baseball cap, the rest of the treatment churn was as difficult.

When you are a cancer patient, this world is hell, and you just hope the result is worth the process. One of the women with whom Dervs shared a treatment room was complaining about hot flashes. Dervs said, "I've been told that this treatment smacks you right into menopause."

"But I'm only thirty-one," the woman said, "and I have a year-old baby."

There was the man who had worked in a chemical plant for years, on the cleanup detail. He said he slogged around chemicals daily, and twenty years later, his body was riddled with cancer and the company he had worked for had been bought out by a bigger one, so was no longer in business.

A beautiful, well-dressed woman in her late forties told Dervs she had four wigs because this was the third time she had lost her hair. Her eyebrows were tattooed on. She said she made that decision because she was tired of looking in the mirror and seeing a cantaloupe look back.

Dervs told the woman and her daughter, who was accompanying her, that Wally was freaked out by her baldness. The daughter said, "I'm thirty-three, and it freaks *me* out."

While she was having cancer treatment, Dervs entered a study at the University of California at San Francisco hospital examining whether exercise during chemo helped to combat fatigue. Why she did this is anybody's guess. She was already overloaded taking care of herself, Wally, Arthur. Maybe she was trying to be some kind of cancer hero herself.

On the other hand, it may have been a way for her

to make friends with the black dog. Some days she thought of cancer the way she thought of Wally's cystic fibrosis. In the person who is Wally, there are hundreds of wonderful aspects and there is cystic fibrosis. That disease is part of who Wally is, and as his parent, Dervs has to embrace that too. In that way, she is trying to embrace the black dog, as part of who she is, something that she has to endure and that can't be separated from her.

Dervs also thought that if the cancer came back, maybe not once but a number of times, she would ultimately refuse treatment, go to Machu Picchu, the Galápagos, Paris instead.

Frustrated, grumpy, looking in the mirror at a clothing store and what's looking back is a bloated, constipated, hairless, sweating because it is 100 degrees outside, miserable person. And I should be happy. Really, I should be. I got a phone call earlier today telling me that I'd received a Lannan Foundation Writing Residency in Marfa, Texas. I can stay from two weeks to a month at a time of my choosing. I about jumped out of my skin, I was so excited. I can go to Marfa and write. That sounds so much like heaven to me right now, yet here I am driving myself crazy because I look bad. I am afraid that it is so hot this wig will melt off my head, and I will be hairless with wig strands hanging off my nose and sliding down my cheeks. A Lannan grant with wig strands.

Pablo Picasso said, "Everything you can imagine is real."
I feel as if everything I couldn't begin to make up is real.

I am driving to the Cancer Center today, down Ashby
toward Shattuck, when the light at Telegraph and Ashby
turns red. There is a white, late-model Lexus in front of
me before the light. I stop behind it, and after about thirty
seconds I must start zoning out because my Volvo drifts
into the Lexus, not hard; it was drifting from a stop. As
soon as it happens, a seventyish-looking woman, thin,
chic, and wearing a neck brace pops out of the Lexus and
starts screaming at me.

"That was quite a jolt, young lady!"

I suggest we get through the light as cars are lining up
behind us, and then stop to exchange information. When
we do, I see there is a passenger in her car, a seventyish
man holding a cane straight up in front of him.

"That was quite a jolt," the woman says again. "We
were already on our way to a medical appointment, and
you did this to us. You must have been driving pretty fast
when you hit us."

"I wasn't driving at all," I say. "I was stopped behind
you, and as you can see, there are only two little dimples
in your bumper from the bolts in my license plate."

*Oh, fuck, she's going to try to say I injured them. This is
an insurance scam waiting for me to drift into.*

"I don't know what you were doing, young lady, but
that was quite a jolt."

I can tell this woman is not injured. There is no damage at all to my car, but I have a feeling it's going to end badly. I sit in the Cancer Center, thinking I should call Arthur. Even though the woman hadn't said that either she or her husband was injured by the impact, I can see it coming.

And I am right. When I get home, call my insurer and am referred to a claims agent, it turns out there is already a claim number, and this woman is indeed alleging that both she and he suffered neck, back, and soft-tissue damage.

*Diogenes, I am on your team.*

When I tell the claims agent that the woman was wearing a neck brace, he tells me this not a good sign because it will be very hard to dispute her claim. So now I have to take my car to be appraised, even though there is no damage to it, thank you, Volvo, and I have to deal with whatever else this tiny accident is going to dish out. The irony is not lost on me that this woman will get more from me for denting her bumper than we did from Christopher Adney for destroying our lives.

I have to wash my wig.

I meet Ann for breakfast at the Blackberry Bistro; she said she wanted to get together before my birthday, which is later this week. She tucks into eggs and smoked salmon and I into challah French toast. Even though my taste buds have gone off duty during the chemo, I savor the textures and sweetness of the bread and syrup in my mouth. As the toast is assaulting my membranes, looking for some taste buds that will get it, Ann hands me a package.

"Your birthday present," she says.

I unwrap a carved wood kachina, about ten inches tall, that looks like a beaver, pigment-dyed, with feathers sticking out of its head.

"Is it a beaver?" I ask.

"Yep. It's a black beaver kachina — Hopi — to bring you good health. It's carved from the dried roots of the cottonwood tree. This is to replace Job. Job is gone."

Job. I'd forgotten him. On one of my trips to Tucson about ten years ago, I found Job. He was an outsider art piece, painted on old fence boards. I had bought him as a present for Arthur, who was never quite a fan but was gracious about accepting this Old Testament Job, tormented, with the devil at his feet, trying to tempt him to veer away from a god who specialized in pestilence and suffering. The day of my cancer diagnosis, Ann came over and said, "I need to take Job out of here."

"Okay, if you need to," I said.

"I do," she said, and took the six-foot-high Job away

from his corner near the fireplace. "This is bad magic. I've always thought so. Steve and I will get rid of him."

I learned later that they had kicked him into splinters behind the piano shop where Steve works and then burned the splinters. Job is gone. Welcome black beaver.

Maybe it was Job that caused me to have this image of myself as a piece of burnt and twisted ash hanging from a hook in the air. This in my last meeting with Charlotte. I think I prefer invisibility to the hanging ash. Charlotte gets back to my mother on this, making a connection between the hanging ash and an infant or even a fetus. Where she goes is that even as a child I knew that my mother wanted to kill me; I knew I was in physical as well as psychic danger. There are truths that, while we may know them, are much more difficult to face in the light.

But enough about me: Cherise and Geoff are getting married. Geoff proposed on July 3, and the next day Cherise walked into my house and extended her left hand.

"So, Johnson, what do you think?"

She has always called me Johnson, as have several other people I love, including my ex-husband and sometimes Arthur.

"Whoa, that is one beautiful ring. The platinum is fabulous against your skin," I say.

Cherise's skin is the color of a perfect latte.

"I thought so too. It's an estate ring, so it wasn't as expensive as a new one and I like the older settings. Listen, Geoff and I want to ask you something, and I want you to feel free to say no, okay?"

"All right."

"As you know, we don't have too much money to spend on the wedding, especially since we spent a fair amount on this ring, so we were wondering if we could have our wedding and reception here, at your house. We would do all the work. You wouldn't have to do anything. Talk to Arthur and see what you think—and don't be afraid to say no."

"Are you kidding? We would love to have your wedding here. I will ask Arthur, but my guess is he will be as excited about this as I am. It's about time we have a celebration here."

I look around at the large combined space of our dining and living rooms and through the glass of the double doors leading out onto the deck.

"We could have musicians at the end of the room by the fireplace, move furniture, have flowers everywhere. It will be great," I tell her.

"Don't get ahead of yourself," says Cherise. "And the deal is, you promise to do none of the work. Nothing. No setup, no cleanup. Nothing."

"Okay, okay, but you can't stop me from planning."

Arthur left this afternoon for four nights in San Francisco to attend a convention and a board meeting for his law firm. He's staying in a hotel because the meetings start early and end late, and he doesn't have the stamina to drive back and forth. Some days you can get caught on the Bay Bridge for hours, and he doesn't want to take the chance. This is it: he is making his first big move to get back to his working life. Although he has been going to the office a couple of days a week and has been regularly advising the lawyers on briefs since he got out of the hospital, four days in a row with a hectic schedule is new. He is so excited about the possibility of being able to do what he used to, even partially, that the adrenaline rush should keep him going. My hope is that the joy his friends and colleagues experience just seeing him functional will override any concerns they have about how he looks or the way he moves in his refashioned body.

He asked me to meet him in the city Tuesday evening to go to a dinner and party his firm is hosting. I realize that I have nothing to wear that matches a swollen face topped by a red wig. Of course, perhaps the same goes for me as for Arthur: people would be happy just to see I'm not dead. That gives one some leeway in dressing, but I still can't go.

Arthur comes back this afternoon after his stay in San Francisco. He calls me from his car driving home and says, "Do you want the headline?"

"Okay."

"I danced last night!"

I am in the grocery picking up a bottle of Odwalla Strawberry Smoothie for Wally, and as Arthur says this, my arm bumps and stops midair as if it has been jolted then frozen. My body shudders as a wave of anger and hurt whirls through it. I hang up the phone.

When Arthur gets home, he asks me what happened, and I say, "I guess the connection got cut off. Maybe you were on the bridge or something."

He is so excited, asking if I want the details.

"Sure, who did you dance with?"

"Adele and Leslie and Rikki — did I tell you she and Eric came to the party? — and other people, not really partnered up, but dancing nevertheless."

"That's wonderful," I say, without enthusiasm.

"What's wrong? I thought you'd be excited for me."

"Oh, I am. It's just that you've been asking Dr. Coufal over and over, 'When will I be able to dance with my wife?' And then, when you are finally at a place and time when you might be able to dance, you don't think for a minute about how your wife is sitting at home with cancer taking care of your kid while you are out dancing. Instead of waiting until we were together, you just go right ahead and dance without me. You are unbelievably selfish! I hope you had a great time. Go screw yourself!"

Arthur's face starts melting and then sets in a grimace.

"I thought you'd be happy," he says, "and instead of congratulating me, all you can do is tell me what I did wrong. Screw you, too."

*I get done with this cancer shit, I'm out of here. I am so out of here.*

At my next appointment with Charlotte, I tell her about Arthur's dancing extravaganza. I also tell her that at one point he said to me, "No matter what, I will always love you and we will get through this."

Charlotte says, "He is such a — "

I interrupt her. "I hope you are going to say *asshole.*"

This is the problem with marriages, partnerships, dog walking groups, neighborhood lemonade stands: when the participants get into an argument, everything each of them says and feels can be true. The question is: can the membership survive the individual truths? Add to this the brain injury factor and the ice thins.

Arthur thought Dervs should congratulate him for dancing. He thought she would be delighted. There he was out on the floor with his eye patch and his cane, moving to a beat beyond the one pulsing in his brain, joining his friends and humanity in a dance after eleven months in stasis. It was exhilarating and he felt triumphant. Not only was no one else having to take care of him, he was making jubilation on his own.

And there was Dervs, frustrated, feeling misunderstood and taken advantage of, ignored, burrowing into hurts of memory, as she sat at home, a captive of cancer treatment, and even so, making sure the home fires were burning as Arthur was burning up the dance floor.

After you get beyond the basic human needs of food and shelter, things get messy.

One year from the accident.

I am having a *Psycho* moment. Sunday's *San Francisco Chronicle Magazine* cover: "Fall Fashion Goes Hitchcock." Alfred Hitchcock was on the thirty-two–cent stamp. What a tease. Hitchcock is the glass of milk Cary Grant carries up a long flight of stairs to Joan Fontaine in the film *Suspicion.* The glass, lighted from the inside, draws our attention, focuses our thoughts on whether this is the vehicle for poison, whether it is Grant's method for murdering his wife. Hitchcock materializes anxiety.

I think my eyebrows are lighted from within. I draw them on crookedly most mornings, as if I were Lobster Boy, the carnival freak, part of the sideshow that winters in Gibsonton, Florida. Lobster Boy, his hands and feet malformed as large claws, was the victim of ectrodactyly syndrome, a hereditary birth defect. Known as a mean son of a bitch, Grady Stiles, a.k.a. Lobster Boy, was shot to death in November of 1992. A mean son of a bitch would draw my eyebrows on crookedly.

On Sunday we drove up the coast to Bodega Bay to hang out, walk the beach, dig in the sand. This is the town where Hitchcock's film *The Birds* was shot in 1963. We stopped at the Tides Wharf Restaurant to eat lunch and buy Wally a sweatshirt because he forgot his, and we found actress Tippi Hedren signing autographs in the crowded lobby. The town was celebrating the fortieth anniversary of the film.

It's been nearly a month since I had my last chemo,

and I'm trying to get myself ready for my "staging operation." Dr. Stern says he is going to check my lymph nodes, take a dozen or so tissue samples from all over my abdomen, clean up anything that looks hinky — my word, not his — take out my appendix and omentum, which he describes as a tortilla-like organ hanging over the stomach that pretty much just collects fat. I wonder if it's lighted from within.

The operation is tomorrow at 11:30 a.m., and I am afraid, that kind of afraid that gives you diarrhea, that grates at your intestines and clenches your stomach, possibly even your omentum. Seems to me if this therapy stuff were working, I wouldn't be so wound up about the operation. My emotions and anxieties are bubbling up to the surface, where I am stuck having to deal with them. Why is this preferable to having them buried under a years-in-the-making, well-tested defense structure?

Last night Arthur and I went out for dinner with Ann — her husband, Steve, is out of town — to a little French restaurant on Piedmont Avenue. What was remarkable about the evening was that it was the first time since the accident that Arthur has gone outside without some kind of walking aid — the first time he has walked without crutches, a walker, or a cane, for a year and a month. There he was listing down the street, but he was listing unaided.

He found out yesterday, at a doctor's visit, that the injuries and operations to his legs have cost him over two inches in height. He measured five feet nine inches. He used to be five feet eleven and a half. Arthur says that explains why his pants are dragging.

Nine days out from surgery, and I feel as if I've been beaten by a hundred guys slinging rolled-up carpets; I feel as if I've been slammed in front of a moving car, shoved down a drainage ditch. I should have anticipated this when the anesthesiologist, sporting mutton-chop sideburns, came in to see me before the operation and said, "This is some major surgery you've got going here."

Since the operation I've been having a pizza dream, not a pizza really, but I dream that I am a pizza crust covered with thinly sliced raw fish, and I am spinning away from the center of something, but I don't know what. I am the raw fish pizza spinning off into blackness. I wake up each time I have the dream thinking, *this is not my dream. I don't belong here.*

Right after the surgery, I woke up in a private room. I think Arthur was there. I was pushing the morphine button, but I'm not sure how often. One of the nurses told me it was set to give me a shot every six minutes, but if I needed more I should ask.

I had an IV going for days, I think, because I couldn't eat solid food. I blew up, evolved into a huge, swollen creature, my face a giant cheese pizza — round and white and doughy. I felt as if each cell in my body had grown fifty percent bigger. I knew this to be true when a couple of days after the surgery a woman woke me at five in the morning, got me out of bed, and made me step on a scale she had maneuvered next to me. I was shocked to find that I weighed twelve pounds more than when I had entered the hospital.

Later that morning, I asked a nurse if the IV could be removed. She said not without a doctor's order, but she could lower the hourly input from 100 ml to 25 ml and would ask Dr. Stern later if I could have the IV and the catheter removed. He said sure, and that I could get out of the hospital that Friday if I could pass gas. So it comes to this: all systems depend on evacuation.

Evacuation I know about. I went home on Friday, four days after the operation.

## SATURN DEVOURS HIS SON

Dervs liked to tell people that she had pasted a copy of Goya's painting *Saturn Devouring His Son* on her binder when she was in high school. She said Saturn was her mother. This was a lie. Dervs never pasted that painting anywhere except in a secret notebook she carried around with her as an adult—after her mother had died. She believed that every time she looked at that painting, she killed her mother again, and this gave her satisfaction.

In the shotgun house back in Bethlehem, when she was a child, Dervs watched her mother's weekly ritual. Every Saturday, Dervs's father brought home freshly ground beef from the butcher's. Her mother stood at the Formica counter next to the sink and carefully unwrapped the package. She untied the string and unrolled the brown, crinkling paper until she revealed a mound of freshly ground chuck inside. The first thing she did was bend her neck down to the paper, close to the flesh. Then with the first two fingers and thumb of her right hand, she gently scraped off a bit of the raw meat and smoothed it into her mouth. She closed her eyes and stretched her neck back and smiled.

"Nothing tastes like this," she said, and scooped up more and more of the beef until she ate nearly a quarter of the package weight.

"I have to stop," she said.

Saturn had already eaten his son's right arm and

head and was now chomping the left arm. He held his son in front of him like an ice cream cone. Dervs was certain he had begun by eating his son's head. She envisioned her own face rearranged by the accident, decorated with slits and zags and scrapings, sections of raw flesh and flowing blood all spinning off into blackness. Spinning into the country where a mother tried to devour her child's mind, to cut it into thin slices and throw it as far from her as possible. Spinning back into the womb where the mother tried for the first time to kill the little fish, the little gilled child growing there.

There were entire years when Dervs tried to conjure up good memories of her mother. She came up with one that took place two months before her mother died. It was during the two weeks Dervs came home from Russia to help her mother sort out her death. Dervs and her parents and a friend went out for dinner, and her mother, who rarely drank, had two grasshoppers, maybe three. She was laughing through the meal and when they reached home, she got out of the car and sat down on the curb, her legs sticking straight out into the street. Dervs sat down beside her and looked at her mother's pale green, buttoned-up suit.

"I haven't had this much fun in years," said her mother.

"Maybe you should have been drinking more," said Dervs.

"No, not after what I saw with my father."

"You think your father's alcoholism was its own device? You don't think he was drinking to help him with what was going on in his mind?"

"Oh, no. There was nothing wrong with my father's mind. He was a brilliant man, talented."

"Well, I didn't know him," said Dervs, as she considered that her mother had matched the color of her drinks to her suit, now a sort of milky green in the light of the street lamp.

"It's time to go in," said her mother.

"I'm telling you. Drink more."

Dervs watched her mother stand up, balance perfectly on her bone pumps, and walk across the pavement and up the steps to the front door. She thought, *there isn't enough liquor in the world to drown that woman's pain.*

This is my first day back driving since the operation. Freedom. My lower back has hurt since the surgery as if everything is out of alignment; however, my eyebrows are starting to grow back. My eyelashes are about an eighth of an inch long. My hair, one and a half months after chemo, is still peach fuzz, also an eighth to a quarter of an inch long and coming in at different places, so I look kind of mangy. Last night Wally and I were sitting on the red sofa in the family room reading, and he ran his hand over my head.

I said, "Feels weird, huh?"

"I like the way it feels," he said. "It's soft."

I still feel as if the stuffing has been knocked out of me, and in a way it has. I feel more injured than I did after the car accident and following the cyst removal back in March, and I have a blister at the very top of the incision, which is a vertical line beginning at my navel and extending downward. I don't think this blister is a problem, but I am on the lookout for redness, oozing, pain, fever, exhaustion — signs of infection. My stomach hurts no matter what I do. Wally's pediatrician told me it can take as long as a year to recover from this kind of surgery.

I called Dr. Tracy's office yesterday to see if I could have my port taken out. She wants it to stay in for a month after the surgery in case I develop an infection and have to have IV antibiotics. I've been in a dog fight.

Wally and I are sitting at the table on our deck. He's doing his homework. The sun is bright and hot, and I'm wearing my baseball cap to keep the sun off my head. I want my hair back *now*, and my eyebrows, which look like shadows of their former selves.

I spent a couple hours this morning looking at photos of the accident: the car, Adney's truck, the road, the medics, the firefighters getting Arthur out of the car, each of us in the hospital. Who are these people, the ones in the hospital? They look a little bit like we do, but the woman has a face swollen twice its normal size and the man is covered with blue bandages and has tubes coming out of him everywhere. The little boy in the wheelchair looks sweet and uncomfortable and displaced.

I want to take the pictures in to show Charlotte. Recently, each time I reach her office door I wonder if: 1) I have forgotten the numerical code that opens it, 2) she changed the code and didn't tell me, 3) the door won't open even if I know the code and do everything right. The thought that Charlotte might not want me is no surprise.

My mother had a light brown leather jacket she used to keep on a hanger on the door leading from the kitchen down to the basement. One day my dog Snickers chewed the sleeve of the jacket. When she saw it, my mother's face shrewed into a long nose and beady eyes as she turned on me.

"I can't have anything nice. You ruin everything!"

I was about six when she said that. She must have liked the way it sounded running on out of her mouth because it became her mantra: "You ruin everything. You ruin everything. You ruin everything." I ruined haircuts, piecrusts, cars, furniture, antique vases, coats, streets, marriages, corporations, the fashion industry.

I continue to wear my one dress that works with the incision, which means it doesn't come in contact with the midsection of my body. It is a black jersey tank of a dress with a v-neck. I can't remember buying it or ever wearing it before. It appeared in my closet when I was looking for something to wear to the hospital before the operation, something loose and easy.

Loose and easy is the wind fluttering across a salt marsh, tumbleweeds floating along in the Sonoran desert watched over by ocotillo and saguaro, the way a dog's ears flop when he is playing. Loose and easy is a child and her mother walking along the street in a small town, looking in windows, smiling and satisfied in the company of each other.

Wildfires are burning out of control in southern California — San Diego, San Bernardino, Simi Valley, Thousand Oaks — where my cousins live. And there is fear of fire in the hills here: late-October ninety-degree days, winds, like a tinderbox waiting for the spark, although it might be more precise to say waiting for a lucifer, as matches were at one time called, to be struck. Feels biblical, and have I mentioned that actor-turned-politician Arnold Schwarzenegger will be our new governor in November? Exactly what was Conan? Pre-biblical?

My driving the last couple weeks has been dangerous. I am out of focus, drifting away, as if something in my brain is ready to break open. Part of me feels like a shadow person, so shy it is hiding behind doorways, the person full of pain and fear. Are these the footprints of my unconscious or is this shadow self the conscious one?

My body has only just stopped hurting all the time, and the infection that came from the pus-filled blister seems to be gone.

Last night, when Wally and I had finished reading before bed, he said to me, "If Dad snores or bothers you with noise during the night, you can send him in to sleep with me."

"That's really nice of you to offer, but I like sleeping with Daddy," I say.

"I like sleeping with Daddy too," Wally says.

Arthur and Wally are making part of Wally's

Halloween costume together. He is going to be the Lego Bionicle Rahkshi Vorahk — I think that's right. I'm painting the costume — silver paint on black sweatshirt and sweat pants — and they are concocting the weapon. I hope it is strong and he can wield it for life.

A new year, a new medical procedure. Arthur was scheduled to have surgery today to have his left femur broken, so they can change the angle at which it enters the knee. Dr. Coufal says the angle is off by ten degrees. This adjustment should make it easier for Arthur to walk without loping from side to side. I was supposed to take him at 1:00 p.m. for a 3:00 p.m. surgery, but someone from scheduling called yesterday afternoon and told us to be at the hospital at 11:15 this morning, that the surgery had been moved up to 1:15. And this morning at ten o'clock, someone called to say the surgery had been postponed for a day, and we would be notified if something changed. At 1:30 we got another call saying we should come in right away, so we piled ourselves and Arthur's bag into the car, arrived near 2:00 and Arthur was in surgery by 3:15, very near the originally scheduled time. Who could make this up?

I don't know what was going on, but all the other surgeries had been cancelled. I'm convinced that only Chris Coufal's schedule and influence got Arthur in and operated on today. All the changes made Arthur very anxious. I could tell this because he was yelling at me about where to drop him off for the surgery, where I had to park, what I had to bring into the waiting area with me. When we arrived in pre-op, there was only one other person there, a woman who had not received the message that her surgery had been postponed. I heard the nurse tell this woman that if she couldn't get back home, she might have to spend the night in the recovery room.

As for Arthur, his surgery took about four hours. It was me and the fish floating around in the aquarium room until Dr. Coufal came in to tell me everything went well. After he got out of recovery, Arthur was taken up to his room, where Dr. Coufal stopped by about ten o'clock at night to check on him. I know this man has three children. When does he get to go home?

*

Here's what happens: When you have a long-term, extensive trauma, everyone gets used to living in trauma space. You get used to the abnormal. This struck me in the middle of the night. I brought Arthur home from the hospital yesterday about noon. He immediately went to bed because he hadn't been able to sleep much in the hospital, and he slept most of the afternoon. I woke him about five o'clock to see if he wanted to get up, have something to eat, talk to Wally. He did, and we managed to get him motoring on his crutches again.

I was happy about having Arthur back, feeling the presence of his body in the bed, knowing he had made it through one more operation, one more round. But last night, Arthur wasn't able to get comfortable, had to sleep on his back and then kept rolling from side to side, like having a log rolling around in bed with you. The log rolls into you, you wake up. The log rolls away, it moves the bed. About 1:30 a.m. the log turned on the light and started to read because it couldn't sleep. This is what I mean about getting used to trauma space. For a moment, I considered it normal that someone would get up in the middle of the night and turn on the light to read, and then I thought *what's going on here?* I went to the guest room.

Wally was up at the same time, going into the bathroom. He said "Mommy" in a plaintive, five-year-old way that allowed me to catch a glimpse of the younger child he had been.

"I've been dreaming, Mom. I've been dreaming that Uncle John and Chris keep giving me presents, and all the presents are burritos. I like burritos, but each new present was another burrito."

Then he opened the bathroom door, went in, and shut it behind him.

I went to sleep thinking about carpets on the floor of my head. I drew a Persian carpet there, then a rag rug, a braided one, Tibetan. I furnished the inside of my skull with carpets. Then I walked into the room with a broom and tried to clean up. The carpets were covered with dried leaves. I was trying to remove the leaves and straighten the edges of the rugs, but the rugs kept crumpling in new ways, new leaves appeared. Trauma has a room of its own in my head.

*Lord of the Rings III: The Return of the King.* Long movie. After sitting through it with Arthur, Wally, and Wally's friend, Morgan, we get up and walk out on our way to Zza's restaurant for pizza. I have a strange, tingling sensation running up and down the inside of my left thigh that won't go away. I think I can walk it out, but it walks with me. What the heck is this now? Last week I had a rash that kept spreading over my body, beginning with my neck, chest, and forearms and then moving to my left calf. I finally went to the doctor on Friday, and the nurse practitioner couldn't identify it, so asked a doctor. She came back and said it could be autoimmune disease, which is not uncommon after treatment for ovarian cancer. I have to see a dermatologist Monday to make sure it's not vascular related. I can repeat what they tell me, but I have no idea what any of it means and I'm not about to look it up on the Internet. Whatever I find there will scare me more.

Recently, a number of people remind me of the animated character Shrek. Who ever knew there were so many big, green trolls out there?

Okay, I'm not dying this week, at least not from the rash or the pain in my leg. The dermatologist said the rash was just contact dermatitis, common, could be from anything, cured with a cream she gave me to put on it. Dr. Stern told me the pain in my leg is caused by a lymphocele — a cyst filled with lymphatic fluid, totally benign, can be resolved by being drained. I can have that done now or wait until I get back from Marfa, my Lannan Foundation residency, which is scheduled for May. I am going to wait. I can't be draining while Arthur is still healing from his latest surgery.

## THE BIG THROWOUTSKI

Arthur and Dervs were working hard to change their circumstances. They believed this would happen, in part, if they got rid of the accoutrements of their illnesses. It was Arthur's idea: the big throw out. He wanted to heave away those objects that reminded him of being in pieces. He began with his cut-off shoes.

"I can't believe I wore these shoes for so long," Arthur said. "And you know what? I don't even remember when I started having to wear them."

"The big toe on your right foot was smashed and they pinned it together. Dr. Wyzykowski did it while you were at John Muir, and there was a big pin sticking out the top of your toe, so we had to cut off the tops of a couple pairs of your shoes to accommodate the pin. You don't remember this?" Dervs said.

"Vaguely. I guess I do and I don't. That was before my mind came back?"

"The operation was before that, yes," said Dervs.

"I remember needing someone to help me get the shoes on, mostly you, that was. I hated it. Hey, remember *The Big Lebowski*?"

Dervs and Arthur had laughed their way through that Coen brothers film together.

"I should have had the John Goodman character—What was his name?—get me a toe. That would have been easier."

"I think his name was Walter. Remember the bowling? Maybe there is a nine-toed bowlers tournament," Dervs said. "You might have qualified for that."

"I am *exiting a world of pain*," said Arthur, throwing the black shoe into a trash bag, then moving on to a pair of pants that had been slit up the side.

"You might still need those," said Dervs.

"I have the ones I'm wearing now and two more pairs with the snaps on the side. That should be enough. I want these ugly things out of my closet."

What he wanted was to have his pre-smashed and pre-operated-on body back. He wanted this new body to leave with the ugly clothes. He wanted the old familiar body, the one that walked straight without aid.

Dervs believed that Arthur sometimes had hated her for being there in those long months following the accident, even though he needed her help. She thought he wanted her to stop being tired and cranky and impatient with him.

But he didn't feel that way. He wasn't aware of resenting Dervs at all, although he did want to have to stop pretending everything was going to be all right, even though he was afraid that if they stopped pretending, their world would disintegrate, and they wouldn't be able to pull it together at all. He did hate Dervs for knowing that, for knowing that this was too much for anyone to bear.

"Okay," said Dervs. "I'm giving away the whole damn collection of hats I bought when my hair started to fall out. Look at this red one. Why did I ever think I would wear a can of tomatoes on my head? And that nobody would notice there was no hair under it? What was I thinking?"

"I don't know," said Arthur. "Maybe you were just under stress and you weren't thinking at all. Maybe all the negative energy made you buy stupid-looking things."

"Maybe I'm just an asshole," said Dervs. "Want to go get an In-and-Out Burger?"

They couldn't get rid of it, all the medical gear; some of it was still in use. When the carpet cleaner came on the Monday after the throw out, he asked about the handicapped toilets, the extra railings on the stairs. Dervs told him about the accident, and after he listened to her abbreviated tale, he said, heaving the steamer in front of him, "You were lucky. Look at you; you're standing here telling me about this terrible thing that happened and you're smiling. That's lucky."

Dervs was thinking that, if she was lucky, this was one fucked-up world. She was thinking that if it hadn't been for Wally, she would have bought a ticket out. Instead she bought a ticket for Hawaii. She bought three: they were going on vacation.

I am in Hawaii. I am in paradise. I am in the waiting room of an after-hours clinic in a fancy hotel in Maui. Wally's right ear and the right side of his face belong to André the Giant. They are huge, swollen, discolored. He is in pain, pain that's killing him, he says. Otherwise, he seems to be all right, but at this moment, otherwise doesn't count.

We only have to wait about fifteen minutes to see the doctor, with his dark hair and wearing a white coat, and who is very nice, and calm. Did I mention calm? This helps me to settle down, allows some of my panic to fall to the floor. The doctor asks what was Wally doing before this happened?

"He was sitting on the grass with a friend, watching the sunset."

"No, Mom, we were lying on the grass talking," says Wally.

He turns to the doctor.

"Can you make the pain stop?"

"Okay. This is a reaction to a bite, and what I don't know for sure is whether the bite was from a scorpion or a centipede," says the doctor. "It could be either, and we can treat it pretty easily. You just have to watch out for further symptoms for a day or so."

The doctor is checking Wally's heart and lungs, asking him to breathe deeply through his mouth. Again Wally says the pain is killing him.

"You have scorpions in Maui? Centipedes bite?" I say.

From living in Tucson, I know about scorpions, but biting centipedes are new to me.

"Yes, we have scorpions, and yes, the centipedes are large and have venomous bites," the doctor tells me.

So why isn't this information in the tourist brochures?

"How big are the centipedes?" I ask.

"Oh, they're big. They can get maybe eight inches long. I've heard longer. They're pretty ubiquitous on the Islands. What you have to do here is give your son some Benadryl for the allergic reaction. That should take down the swelling. I can also write him a prescription for pain, and I'll give you a couple pills for tonight because you won't find a pharmacy open. There is a drugstore up the road where you can get Benadryl."

Wally is clutching Wolfie; I am clutching Wally; Arthur is clutching me. We are the vacationing family.

"Why did this have to happen to me?" says Wally.


Hawaiian centipedes, I learn, have forty-two legs, one on each side of twenty-one body segments. They are dark green, long and flat, with brown heads. The heads have antennae, although who could see the antennae for the legs. Under the head is where the jaws hide. The set of hind legs is larger than the rest, so they can hold prey in them while chomping.

I was about the same age as Wally is when I saw my first centipede. My mother and I were in the dining room, the middle downstairs room of our shotgun house. It was a Friday night; my father was working the three-to-eleven shift at the steel, which is how he referred to the mill, and my mother was teaching me how to clean. Her version of cleaning was to attack; she attacked dirt and dust everywhere, cleaned everything. Everything included windows, blinds, drapes, floors, baseboards, corners up and down, furniture, knickknacks, under the furniture, above the windows, the ceiling. She was the woman who ran her finger over the surface of a slat at the top of a window blind to check for dirt.

This was one of my first lessons, and my mother was instructing me on how to dust. I was to take each tchotchke off the dining room table and wipe it off with a damp rag. Then I was to wipe the table with a dry rag, starting with the top and going down the sides and the legs to the floor. I was doing one of the legs when my mother screamed and jumped on the sofa.

"Kill it! Kill it!" she yelled, pointing at the floor.

I stood up and saw a long, thin, light-brown bug with what seemed like a million legs running across the floor. How could a creature have this many moving appendages?

"Take your shoe off. Hit it with your shoe! Now!"

My mother's voice was getting higher and louder. And I did what she wanted. I got my shoe off, flew across the floor and smashed that centipede into a puddle of legs and ooze. I had never seen anything like this insect, never knew they existed. And now I had to clean up the ooze before my mother would get down off the sofa.

That was it for my cleaning lesson. My mother was out of that room for the night even though one of her rules was that the house had to be cleaned on Friday. No one was allowed to do anything on the weekend until the house was clean. As I got older, I realized that one of my jobs was to clean and another was to kill the insects and creatures that scared my mother: centipedes, spiders, worms, wasps, bees, moths, ants. When I heard a certain scream, it was my cue. I began to see the bugs as extensions of her, as having come out of her, escaped from their cages inside her mind. I think that's what she believed too.

Don't get me wrong, I love my family, but for nearly a week I have been alone, writing, in Marfa, Texas, staying at one of the Lannan Foundation houses, and I am really happy. I got here because of my poems, but I find myself writing prose, writing about the accident. I am reading Nicanor Parra: "He's trying to figure out a way to say it, so he can survive."

I walk the desert and get some time to think about this experience with Charlotte. Among her mantras are: "There is no time in the unconscious" and "Pronouns have no meaning," which I think translates into pronouns can refer to multiple people, have multiple antecedents, at the same time. I can't write about it in prose. Poetry allows more room for movement, ties you down less, is fluid, not so much nailed in a moment. Poetry gives a writer more room to address what we don't have language for.

Another aspect of a poem is to encourage a lot of people in this country — where we have almost no poetry education — to turn the page, ignore the black spots forming letters, forming words. Poems encourage Americans to run for the hills. And this includes my husband, who, early in our marriage, came home one evening saying he was stressed out and had a headache.

"I know what will make you feel better. It always works for me," I said.

I went to get him a cold washcloth and selected a book of poetry by Emily Dickinson.

"Lie down here," I said, patting the living room sofa.

"Wow," said Arthur, "thanks."

"Put the washcloth on your forehead, covering your eyes too. And just lie back and listen. This will help you relax."

I started reading:

"Hope" is the thing with feathers —
that perches in the soul —
And sings the tune without the words —
And never stops — at all —

"Wait a minute," said Arthur. "You have to stop."

"Why? Don't you like it?"

"It's not that I don't like it, but I can tell already that I'm working to figure out what it means and that's making me even more stressed. I'm really sorry, but this isn't relaxing to me. I'm sorry."

"You don't have to figure out what it means. Just listen to it."

"I can't do that," said Arthur. "I'm worried you'll want to talk about it and I'll get it wrong."

"You can't get poetry wrong," I say. "You get from it what you get."

"Well, I don't get it," he said.

"Okay. That's it for you and poetry, I guess."

*Shit. How could I have married somebody like this?*

THERAPY

First the lung rises slowly,
dressed in a red suit. Then a bright helicopter,
sourcebooks riffling. Everyone is eager
except the woman waiting, the hole
dissolving her mouth. Like Alice
everything becomes smaller, smaller
just to know how it feels — evaporation
or love. The vial contains ground glass

and nails. She hangs a sliver of *the Inferno*
around her neck and drinks it in with a straw.

Arthur and Wally just left after spending two days with me in Marfa. They are driving back to El Paso and flying via Southwest from there to Oakland. I miss them even though I want to be here writing. I felt sad waving them good-bye, seeing my son through the glass of the car window. Arthur with his cane and eye patch, getting on the planes, renting a car for the three-hour drive here, Arthur whom I get mad at when he is short-tempered. I get prickly with him, don't feel like such a good companion.

The other prickle in my life is this damn lymphocele, which seems to be causing more trouble. I have this leg thing and a pain in my lower back that was just a little bit when I saw Dr. Stern but now is constant. This makes me worry about what else could be going on. At one point Dr. Tracy said something about nonspecific abdominal ailments being a sign of spreading ovarian cancer. She was talking in general, but I took the phrase and ran with it, right to the sign in my head that reads *Go Nuts Here*.

I have been obsessed with Lucy Grealy lately. The writer Ann Patchett published a book, *Truth and Beauty*, about their friendship. After I read that, I reread Lucy's book, *Autobiography of a Face*. I can't believe she endured as long as she did; she was thirty-nine years old when she died. This is a woman who had a facial cancer when she was a child, and the radiation treatment was so severe that she spent the rest of her life having her face rebuilt and rebuilt and rebuilt because the radiation had made permanent reconstitution impossible. This was a woman who wore her medical problems on her face in a country where appearance is everything. I knew her briefly one summer when we were both teaching for the Johns Hopkins Center for Talented Youth at Dickinson College, and I was in awe of her then. When I feel sorry for myself, I think about her. I want to stop walking around with fear all the time. I want to stop walking around expecting the next bad thing, which makes me think I should get this cyst drained sooner than I anticipated. I think I will make some phone calls tomorrow, see if I can get a surgery date, and then see if the Lannan Foundation will let me come back if I leave early.

On my morning walk today, I saw a red fox, a roadrunner zipping across the road, and I found a perfect and dead Monarch butterfly, which I picked up and brought back to the house with me. I taped it onto the inside cover of my journal. It is so beautiful I need to take it with me.

I've been watching the barn swallows that have nested just under the roof of the front porch here. There are four young birds, and the parents work all day feeding them. Just after the small ones hatched, the parents returned with food quickly. Now the adult birds are gone longer, I suppose going farther for food, or if they are like humans, stopping at the coffee bar to take a break from the chaos and constant demands at home. When they return, the little mouths open and the parents let the food drop so quickly that I haven't been able to catch it with my camera. But what a gift to have them living right next to the door.

Tomorrow I say good-bye to this house for now. I woke up in the middle of the night Thursday with intense pain in my lower back and decided I have to go home to deal with this cyst. It's 2:30 in the afternoon, and I have to print this journal entry out, so I can pack my printer and also find out if I'm going to need to mail anything before the post office closes.

I was originally scheduled to go home on the ninth, three days before Cherise's and Geoff's wedding. Maybe my being home earlier will give me the chance to help them get the house ready, which I hadn't expected to be able to do. My cyst drainage is scheduled for next Thursday.

Back in Alta Bates hospital, in Interventional Radiology, where they insert a catheter into my abdomen to drain this damned lymphecele. These buggers are apparently pretty common after lymph nodes are dissected during pelvic surgery. Here's the deal: I have a tube sticking out of the right side of my abdomen, attached to the tube is a bag, which I attach with tape to my right thigh, into which the fluid from the lymphocele will drain. I have to measure the amount of drainage, which the docs say will decrease pretty soon, and when the cyst is fully drained, the tube comes out. I think I'm looking at a couple weeks. I'm back to wearing loose skirts. I only have a couple of those, so I hope this works quickly.

I'm supposed to come back in a week, to see how the drain is proceeding.

Again I'm in the aquarium room at John Muir, waiting for Arthur to come out of surgery. I was supposed to be having my drain checked today, and instead I am here. On Sunday, Arthur told me something was wrong with his left leg. He said it felt like something changed and was causing him pain, but he couldn't identify what that was. He got an emergency appointment with Dr. Coufal on Monday, and sure enough, the metal rod in his femur had snapped. He is now in emergency surgery to repair it.

Ann tells me she thinks the real reason I came back from Marfa early was that somehow Arthur's body and my body communicated when we saw each other, and mine knew I had to get home because something was going to happen to Arthur's. In my former life, I would have laughed at this notion; now, I'm not so skeptical. I have learned that we communicate in ways we don't even know about or can't pinpoint or know how to track, so I'm not laughing at any of it.

Arthur will be in the hospital a couple of days. I will have my cyst checked tomorrow, although it seems to be producing a lot of fluid, and I don't see a reduction in the amount I have been measuring in a glass kitchen beaker. I thought I would only have to do it once a day, at night, but I'm emptying the darn thing several times a day. I've emptied it into Coke cans, water bottles, anything at hand. Slosh, slosh — that's what I sound like walking around. I try to appear cool while sloshing, like the noise must be coming from somebody else, kind of what we did about farts in fifth grade.

Our house is a festival site. Cherise and Geoff are getting married this afternoon, and Cherise and her friends spent the week decorating the house and front garden and back decks with flowers and planters. There is so much color that it feels as if we are in the middle of an extravaganza. Pools of purple hydrangeas flood the front, trellised garden. Baby's breath and freesia and calla lilies have popped up in pots and vases throughout the house. Ivy is twining everywhere. I have enjoyed people strolling in and out, placing beauty; they have created more light, more air.

The ceremony will take place on the front deck between the small, terraced garden and the house. I'm worried that it will be too hot for Cherise's grandparents, who are in their eighties. But Birdie and Willie, with whom Cherise lived for much of her time growing up, would endure the heat of the Sahara to be here today.

Arthur is home, just barely, after his surgery, getting around on his crutches, frustrated by not being able to contribute more. It's making him a little crazy that Geoff and his friends have to move furniture around without his help. I am hoping he has the fortitude to get through the ceremony and reception without collapsing. He must feel as if he spends his life on crutches, recovering from one cut or another.

The caterers have arrived with their crates and boxes and knives. I always imagine caterers carrying extremely sharp knives. Cherise and Geoff decided to offer desserts at the reception rather than a huge meal at four in the afternoon. Now chocolate cakes, cookies, piles of fruit, cheese plates, the wedding cake — adorn all available surfaces. And there will be wine, champagne, coffee, and cold drinks. They are setting up drink stations in the dining room and on the back deck.

Rachel, the minister, got here about an hour ago and is going over the ceremony with us. Ann and I and some other friends have pieces to read. We need to be cued about when to do that. Otherwise, it will be pretty straightforward and short. We worried about people figuring out where to park because our house is on a hill and there are no sidewalks, but everyone seems to be managing without much trouble. Cherise is getting ready to disappear to put on her dress. That was my wedding present to her, the dress. We went to a vintage store, and although the ivory gown isn't vintage, the headpiece — made of pearls and satin — is from the 1920s and perfect. Cherise is not a shy, retiring woman. She is tall, gorgeous, and assertive, a woman who attracts attention even when it's not her intent. Today, she intends it.

The guests are as colorful as the flowers — from skin tone to dresses and hats. Some of Geoff's family members are pale and blond, and some of Cherise's family have dark brown skin, and the rest of us fill in the spectrum between. We are black and white and Hispanic and mixed ethnicities, and today we are all stunning.

After the ceremony begins, it is over in ten minutes, and all seventy-five of us head inside. Ann's husband,

Steve, is a musician, and he and a friend are playing the piano and guitar. People are on the back deck that stretches across the length of the house; they are in the dining and living rooms; some have gotten drinks and dessert and gone back out to the front. Arthur and I stop to put our arms around each other, mostly that's me putting my arms around him, circumnavigating the crutches. We look at each other with silly grins. He's hobbling and I'm draining and it doesn't matter. This is a good day.

The drainage gig isn't going so well. After a couple weeks of nonstop lymphatic fluid flowing out the hole in my abdomen, the doctors decided to try a more aggressive approach. They now pump alcohol into the lymphocele, I roll on a table from side to side, getting the slosh going, and then they take out the alcohol. I had my third alcohol sclerosis, that's what the procedure is called, this morning, and the amount of fluid coming out of me does not seem to be decreasing. How could I be producing all this stuff?

Meanwhile, the leaks continue. The other day I was at East Bay Nursery with two nine-year-olds, buying two rose bushes and two bags of dirt when fluid starts running down my leg into my shoe. My skirt is mid-calf length, so I hope that covers it up. My shoe is squishing, and I know I have to get out of there, so I plow through the line, get the boys to load the car, and take off as fast as possible for home. I feel as if I'm in a horror film: *Night of the Living Lymphocele.* When is this going to end?

At least Arthur is back on his feet, although he is still on crutches. He's going to his office in downtown Oakland to work, has some kind of system rigged up so he can drive. He is working, but I think the physical problems keep him from being at the top of his form.

If it's ten o'clock in the morning, I must be back in Interventional Radiology for another alcohol sclerosis. This is number six. I have appointments Monday, Wednesday, and Friday this week, and the amount of fluid draining is going down. Yesterday it was only 20 milliliters (or ccs?) for the whole day. Still measuring in that kitchen beaker.

And I'm still obsessed with Lucy Grealy. After the onset of her cancer at age ten, came radiation, then chemo, and a seemingly endless number — thirty-eight maybe — of operations over the next thirty years. She died of a drug overdose. Maybe it was accidental, maybe not. But it followed more botched and difficult operations to repair her face. She had tried to kill herself several times, and I can understand that. How much suffering can one person endure? She must have been incredibly angry.

People ask all the time how many operations Arthur has had, and the truth is that neither of us knows. We haven't kept count, and there were several in the hospital in Bend about which neither of us were cognizant. That first week after the accident, Arthur was being worked on pretty continually, the doctors trying to put him back together. When something happens in excess, numbers become irrelevant. How many times can a person go through more agony, more medical procedures, and how many times survive it? How much determination does it take to be Stephen Hawking?

The drain came out today. I am a free woman. No more tubes and tape and bags. I can wear pants, shorts, a bathing suit, anything I want. I want to swim. I want to be ecstatic and joyful. And I am. My only sadness is that Cherise and Geoff are moving this weekend, to New Haven, where Geoff is studying for an MBA. Cherise will be working on her dissertation there. I've had her close by for five years, and I don't like this upcoming distance. Moving away always ends in a moving away. I want the daily, the quotidian, the minute-to-minute living with the people I love. That's where the essence of our lives resides. Now I know when Cherise has a headache; I know when she's angry with Geoff; I know if she is having trouble working. I regret losing all those tiny connections that comprise our days. I don't want her to leave me.

Animals know things. Call it intuitive or primitive or instinctual. They know things, and if they are domestic animals, they want to be part of the pack's drama. That's my explanation for why Vinnie jumped off the stairs last night while he was playing with Wally. He jumped off the stairs sideways, which he has never done, and slammed right into the wall outside Wally's room. He howled and cried, and all I could do was hold him and try to settle him down. An eighty-five-pound running dog with a long, broken leg at 9:30 in the evening. One man on crutches, a nine-year-old boy, and me. Since the top floor of our house is our living area, with the bedrooms downstairs, we had to find a way to get Vinnie up two flights of stairs to street level and the car. I ended up rigging a sling from beach towels, with Arthur at one end and me at the other. Arthur held onto the railing with one arm and held the sling with the other; Wally was next to Arthur holding his crutch; I was at the bottom end hoping that nobody fell. I don't know how we did it, but we managed to get Vinnie up to the car and into the back of the station wagon, and then I drove us to the twenty-four–hour vet in Berkeley, where they helped us get him out of the car and took him into the exam area right away.

The doctor came out within the hour to tell us Vinnie's leg was badly broken in several places — both bones, one in pieces. She could set it temporarily tonight and had given Vinnie pain medication that would also put him to sleep. We decided to wait until his leg was stabilized, and she made an appointment for Vinnie to have surgery in the morning. Of course, there is only one veterinary surgeon she would recommend for this kind of complicated work and she had to reach him. We left the office about midnight. All this time, Wally was watching the bullfrog and turtles in the terrarium, making up stories, playing some word games with us and himself.

Here's what I think: Vinnie sensed both Wally and Arthur had broken their legs and he was joining them. You can say that is ridiculous; dogs break their legs all the time. I can go with that too, but my experience since the accident leads me to believe in more than coincidence. I just don't know what. Freud might say it is the unconscious, or perhaps conversation between different beings' unconsciouses. Is that a word?

What is it? *Just when I thought I was out, they pull me back in.*

Just when I got rid of the damn lymphocele and thought I was on to the beach, the tops of my thighs started to swell. I went to Dr. Tracy, who said it was lymphodema — fluid collection that results from the lymphatic system not being able to drain properly, and that I should see an occupational therapist for what to do about it. Upstairs from the Cancer Center are physical and occupational therapists among other medical professionals, so I got an appointment with an OT, and here's what she tells me: it appears I have stage one lymphodema; I will have to learn massage techniques to get the lymphatic fluid to drain; I will have to do these techniques a couple times a day; I will have to wear bike shorts or Spanx to keep the fluid from accumulating, particularly on long rides in planes, trains, and automobiles; on long rides I have to get up and move around at least every two hours; this will probably continue the rest of my life. At this point, I ask her if it can't go away. She tells me she's known of a couple cases of early stage that seem to have gone away, but not to hang any hopes on that. Apparently this is one of those things that flares up, so it might seem like nothing for a while and then the swelling gets worse. Shoot me fucking now.

Arthur calls to say my most recent abdominal CT is fine. I've been an anxious mess, physically and emotionally, since my gynecologist told me she wanted the scan done. She said she felt some dense tissue and wanted to make sure it was scarring and nothing else. Xanax. I've been taking my flying Xanax. I feel as if I am moving through this mess, frame by frame, although being back in Marfa is helping me.

This morning as I was out walking, a tarantula crossed the road ahead of me. I also saw three dead rodents and a bone, which appeared to have cartilage attached. The *American Heritage Dictionary* tells me that tarantism is a "disorder characterized by an uncontrollable desire to dance, especially prevalent in southern Italy from the fifteenth to seventeenth century and popularly attributed to the bite of a tarantula." After I read that, what I see is a tarantula dancing, a whole row of dancing tarantulas, tarantula song and dance teams with tap shoes and high hats, little tarantula canes that some of its feet dance around. Smiling tarantulas dancing across the road. I like tarantulas. At the Desert Museum in Tucson, you can hold them and they will gently step across your hand, each foot-strike a little whisper.

On the Internet, I look up my first boyfriend, Stan, well, my first sexual partner — he was also my boyfriend. Turns out he's pretty easy to find, and at one site I see a picture of him and his wife dipping something out of a kettle. I can't tell what the something is, but his wife looks like his mother, right down to the blonde hair and smile, only his wife is not as tan as his mother used to be. Stan looks pretty much the same but bigger.

## A TRICKLE ON THE FLOOD PLAIN

What Dervs saw of the Rio Grande was a trickle, a dribble, a whisper of the river's former self. Douglas tells her it runs to ground about one hundred miles from the Gulf of Mexico. Douglas, the Lannan representative in Marfa, and his wife, Kristen, took Dervs on a trip down Pinto Canyon Road to the artist Donald Judd's ranch and on to the border, through a landscape scented with acacia and ramadas. What begins as a small stream in the San Juan mountains of Colorado, the river that draws the natural boundary between Texas and the Mexican states of Chihuahua, Coahuila, Nuevo León, and Tamaulipas has become so small at its destination that most years now it cannot lend even drops to the gulf. The summer of 2001 was the first time the Rio Grande failed to make its destination. More users than water, too much damming, a wounded river.

Dervs wondered if the river would ever recover from human intervention. She wondered if she would ever recover from the toxins and knives that had gone into her body. She thought this as she wrote about the accident and as she looked at her body, not just the scars but also her thumb, where a tiny remnant of car metal was lodged between the nail and the first joint and where the skin had formed a bubble over the metal, surrounded it to keep it in place. She had asked Arthur's surgeon about this metal piece, and his response was to leave it alone. What happened during the accident was still a mystery to her; however, as she sat at the table in Marfa writing about being cold and unconscious in the hospital in Bend, she realized she was cold in Marfa. For days she was cold, as if her body had a memory and was back in time with her mind. She got so cold that she went out and bought jeans and a pair of cowboy boots in order to write without shaking.

One evening after she had finished working, she was talking on the phone to Wally when the night tried to come in, so she walked outside with the phone and stood in the middle of the street, describing the sky. She told Wally she saw the dippers and Cassiopeia, his constellation because it has the shape of a W. She described the galaxy swirls against the black sky, how clearly she could see thousands of stars from where she was standing, and then Wally stopped her.

"Mom, I need you to walk inside now."

"Why? Can't you see this?" she said.

"I need you to walk inside because I am getting jealous. I want to be there looking at the sky with you."

The library of Wally's childhood was so big. It contained galaxies and rivers and a father who could withstand the force of a moving truck. Dervs thought about all those summer days she'd walked to the Bethlehem Public Library to learn about the world—Fernwood Street to Wood to Broad to Market and then down the steps to the children's floor and from there to the biographies. She had read them all by the time she was out of fourth grade. She even liked the vestiges of other kids—peanut butter smears, dirt, the occasional dried snot—because that meant she had company in these worlds, these lives to inhabit that were not her own life. Dervs read the books with blue and orange covers and even the green ones that had been read so often they had been re-covered, their riffled edges cut straight and clean.

ARTHUR is spelled out in one-foot-high ice placed in front of a poster stating, "May the Force Be With You."

"You're dripping," I say to Arthur, looking at the sculpture.

"Yes, but how often do you get to see your name in ice? It's worth the wet," he says, waiting for me to groan at the pun.

"Kiss me before the onslaught," I tell him, as our nephews, Chad and Aaron, the first people to see us come in, head toward us. They look handsome, dressed in suits rather than the jeans or basketball shorts we usually see them in. Chad is in his first job since finishing college and Aaron is a college sophomore. They are both grinning.

"Uncle Pippy," says Aaron. "Congratulations."

"Yeah, some party," says Chad. "I hope if I ever work at the same place for twenty years, I get a shindig like this."

"I think they are just surprised I made it twenty years," says Arthur, an arm around each of them. "My board of directors is apparently happy that I'm still alive, not to mention on the job."

The conversation goes unfinished, as many will tonight, given the many people who want to spend a little time with the evening's star. Friends and family members from all over the country have come to roast Arthur on his two-decade anniversary working for Trial Lawyers for Public Justice. In 1984, he was hired as the only staff attorney at an infant public interest law firm, and when the first executive director left three years later, took his place.

Hors d'oeuvres float by on trays, but we have no time to eat. Both our mouths are full of streaming words. I manage to capture a glass of wine and see that Arthur is sipping a Coke between sentences and exclamations. This is my first time back in D.C. since we moved from here to California in 1999. Then I didn't care if I ever returned, but seeing the faces of friends I've missed for five years makes me wistful. D.C. was too conservative for me in many ways, and there was always too much attitude. What that attitude was depended on whom you were talking to. Tonight, however, the talk is all about Arthur.

The program starts shortly after everyone is seated for dinner. According to the thirty-two–page program book, we are "honoring, celebrating, roasting" Arthur and his "20 Years of Commitment to Public Justice." The first presenter is Susan Saladoff, our friend from Oregon. Susan is in Florida at an event for her parents this evening, but she made a video titled *Arthur Bryant: This Is Your Life*. The opening shot is a little boy with a shock of dark, curly hair who, when he is taken for his first pony ride, organizes all the other kids to *Free the Ponies!* and goes on from there in his search for justice.

After Susan, Jeff Foote gets up to speak. His visual aid is a slide show; however, after the jokes, he is serious for a moment: "I've always said that Arthur is the smartest guy I know. And then came the accident and his head injury and his six-week recovery from that and the four-month hospitalization, and the whole time I was watching to see what effect this would have on his mental capacities, and I am happy to be able to say it seems not to have had any, and that Arthur is still the smartest guy I know."

Two of the original TLPJ board members perform a skit about Arthur's job interview for the staff attorney position. One of them, portraying Arthur, wears a curly dark wig and Hawaiian shirt and comes in carrying a bag of potato chips. They ask him about problems with food choices, and he tells them he has no problems, that his favorite foods are hot dogs and milkshakes and chips. He also tells them he calls his friends on their birthdays and sings to them, that he thinks sending birthday cards is important because he is happy the people he loves were born. He says that if he is ever responsible for editing other attorneys' briefs, he will tell them YAAPIER — You Are Absolutely Perfect In Every Respect. He is hail-fellow-well-met, although they do say that when they call one of his law school professors he tells them that "Arthur is a bit of a wiseass when somebody does something dumb."

Paul Bland, one of the staff attorneys, also talks about Arthur's food choices. He says that, left to his own devices, Arthur has the nutritional habits of an unparented eleven-year-old boy. Paul also notes that although many people see Arthur as a visionary, when he edits legal briefs he is obsessed with detail, so much so that one of the other attorneys labels it the Happy-to-Glad Syndrome — which is that if a lawyer has written "happy," Arthur will scratch it out and write "glad," and if the lawyer has written "glad," Arthur will scratch it out and write "happy." After the teasing, Paul concludes by saying that after the accident Arthur was so missed because the "energy and response and life people feel when Arthur walks in the office door is incredible."

When it's my turn to speak, I take an index card with a couple topics written on it to the podium, but I'm not going to forget anything:

> If you look at the inside cover of the program book, you will see a photo of a young and thin Arthur in a gold-lamé jumpsuit with a microphone. Truly, this jumpsuit is gold lamé. This is Arthur as a vocalist for his college band, The Fenders. Now I have to tell you: The Fenders were a cover band of Sha Na Na. That's right, a cover band of a cover band. And who would want to cover Sha Na Na? But the most amazing thing about this picture is how Arthur got all that curly hair slicked back. He told me that after trying all sorts of things, the one product that worked was K-Y Jelly. I am not making this up. Arthur was a K-Y Jelly head. I don't know what that means.
>
> Arthur and I met in court outside Philadelphia in 1981, on his first case after clerking. He was working for a first-amendment law firm in Philadelphia that represented the Philly newspapers. At the time, I was working as a broadcast journalist. A couple years later, when Arthur sued Central High in Philadelphia — an all-boys school with the best reputation in the city — to accept girls, I did a story

on the lawsuit. I was working for a statewide news show called *The People's Business* produced by WQED in Pittsburgh, and I interviewed Arthur as part of the story. When I spoke with him after the story had aired, I expected him to tell me that I had presented the case fairly, but all he wanted to talk about was how the photographer shot him from below and made him look like a squirrel. I have told him in the years since that I am responsible for many things, but if he looks like a squirrel, I have no part in that. He can blame his parents, his diet, but not me.

Ten years after we met, Arthur and I got married, and that's when I noticed that he had no hobbies. Most of us have something we spend time on other than our work and families, but not Arthur. He worked. So I suggested he might like to get a hobby, expand his interests. "Okay," he said. "I can get a hobby. How about cooking? That's a good skill to have."

"Great," I said, particularly because on the nights Arthur was responsible for dinner, we'd have takeout. In truth, before his quest for a hobby, Arthur said he could cook four things: Hot dogs — these he could grill or boil. He could make tuna salad, which for him consisted of canned tuna and mayonnaise. If he wanted a sandwich, he slapped this mixture on toasted wheat bread. He could also make English muffin pizzas. I have to say that I had never heard of English muffin pizzas before Arthur, and if you don't know, these are

English muffin halves dribbled with olive oil, spread with canned pizza sauce, covered with some kind of cheddar cheese, then sprinkled with oregano. They go into a 350-degree oven for fifteen minutes. The fourth meal Arthur said he could cook was barbecued chicken, but I have to say, in the fourteen years we have been married, I have never seen him make this dish.

For his birthday in August of 1994, I bought Arthur a book he requested to pursue his hobby. It was titled *Now You're Cooking*. To the best of my knowledge, he read this book one evening. I do not believe he ever cooked anything from it. However, he did pursue his hobby later that fall when he cracked open the *New York Times Cookbook* to the Caesar salad recipe. He made a good Caesar salad that first night, and he's been making it since. Our son was born at the very end of 1994, so Arthur didn't have much spare time for a couple years.

In 1996, he again took up his hobby. This time because he developed a yearning for his mother's spaghetti sauce. He got his mother to send him the recipe and proceeded to make three batches of it. All in the same year and never since, but it tasted pretty good.

In 2000 Arthur lost a Supreme Court case five-to-four and got so depressed he decided to bake a cake. I don't quite understand the connection, but Arthur baked a killer banana cake — once, only once. It was yummy. Maybe someday he'll make it again.

The real issue here is that Arthur doesn't have time for a hobby. He likes his work so much that he doesn't need one. He always says that this public interest law firm is like a family, and you all proved that after the accident. Thank you for taking such good care of him.

After I finish many more people speak, most unscripted from the floor, friends who want to lend their voices to the chorus singing Arthur's praises. There are stories of how he followed his dream to change the world; of suing a club in Houston for racial discrimination; of his bringing the first Title IX case in the nation, so women could have equal access to sports teams and training. His friend Barry stands up and talks about Arthur in high school in Harrisburg, Pennsylvania, how he played the guitar at school assemblies, wore rainbow-colored suspenders, and loved being the center of attention. Barry says, "Even now, he likes to be the center of attention. This is *my* fiftieth birthday, and I end up spending it at a party for Arthur."

When Arthur finally gets to the microphone he is teary and effusive, and after thanking everyone, tells the story about leaving his job at the first amendment firm in Philadelphia after being offered the staff attorney position at Trial Lawyers for Public Justice. He says that when he told his boss, David Marion, that he was giving notice to take the TLPJ job, David said to him, "How much more can we pay you to stay?"

"You don't understand," said Arthur. "This is a public interest job. I'm taking over a fifty percent pay cut to go there."

"Okay," said David, "then how much less can we pay you to stay?"

When the program concludes, we hang around and talk to as many people as we can. My stepbrothers, John and David, have brought eye patches and don them to have a picture taken with Arthur — the three of them in a row, each wearing a black eye patch, made funnier because John has his on upside down. Back in the hotel room later, we look through the program book at photographs, newspaper clippings, good wishes from hundreds of friends. We are so energized by the evening that it takes us hours to get to sleep — and Arthur can't stop talking about how lucky he is.

Dreams may be the stuff of fiction and nonfiction alike, but I had no intention of including any here until I woke up scared this morning. I know my dreams come from my unconscious, but sometimes I wonder *who is in there?* I feel as if there is a committee giggling and piecing together disparate notions for effect, to see what my reaction will be, perhaps sometimes to communicate with me. But *who are these dream makers in my head?*

I have only a small piece of this dream. I am inside a box made of light-colored wood, plywood maybe, it doesn't feel substantial, or maybe it does. The box is about ten feet long and four feet wide and three feet high, at least that's how it appears from above. (I can see this dream both as actor and audience. Perhaps as actor, I feel it more than see it.) I am lying down and my right arm is chained to the side of the box, so I cannot get up. I really want to move out but can't figure how to, when a blonde female figure walks through a door at the end of the box, a door I hadn't seen, and even though the box is only three feet high, this figure is full size and the door appears to be as well. The figure comes up to me and takes my left hand. I get up, somehow standing in the box, and walk with her out the door. When I look back, the chained figure, me I suppose, is still there even though I am also walking out the door.

I meet with Charlotte later in the day and tell her the

dream. She posits the notion that the box is a coffin — how could I have missed that? — and the chained figure is both my mother and me, which leaves me chained to my mother in her coffin. Charlotte thinks that the female figure leading me out represents her, and that the figure I see still chained when I leave is my mother. I hope she is right. That woman may be my mother, but I want to be rid of her.

Here's another Charlottism: "Psychic reality trumps concrete reality every time." If my unconscious thinks my mother is dead, maybe she is.

I feel desperate, despairing, unhappy. So does Arthur. I don't know what is between us. I have terrible concerns, but none that I can voice or even uncover. Tonight he asks me three questions:

1. Do I love him?
2. Do I think he is responsible for the accident?
3. Am I repulsed by his body now?

I say, "Yes, no, no."

I lie about number three. It's not his body. His body is patchworked, riveted, painted with scars but fine. I have trouble looking at his *face* because I see one eye and one big black patch. I realize only now that for years I counted on his eyes for comfort, and now one of them is a space, an abyss, a black hole, nothing I can use.

How can I tell him this? Charlotte says I am cruel not to. This is not his fault; he didn't do anything wrong to end up with this eye. How can I tell him it unnerves me, takes him away from me, pushes me into my own circle of loneliness? Charlotte tells me I'm cutting myself off from him, creating distance between us, that I don't believe he can be there or we can be there for each other. So here we are: each of us tortured and lonely because I don't speak.

What an asshole I am. Arthur senses there is something I am not saying. All these questions he keeps asking. I realize it's his eye patch I hate. Now I have to tell him.

We are sitting at the kitchen table just after lunch. I have had my usual *Portofino no bread* from the neighborhood Italian deli. Arthur had an Italian sub, or a hoagie as we called them growing up near Philly. I am drinking iced tea, Arthur a Coke.

"Listen," I say. "I have to tell you something. I don't think you're going to like it, but I have to tell you."

"Anything," he says. "What's going on?"

"What's going on is that I have real trouble with your eye patch. I know you can't help it. I know that, but when I look at it, I see nothing but a black hole looking back at me. For the eleven years before the accident, I realize that I looked to you for happiness, comfort, acceptance, joy — all of it. I got those things from looking at your eyes, which sometimes reflected me and sometimes were off on their own adventures, but I got to see what was going on inside you. That was a way we spoke to each other, non-verbal, but immense. And now, I don't have that anymore. I can only see one eye that is trying its hardest to take in everything, compensate for everything. I feel lonely because I can't look at you."

Arthur takes a sip of his drink and starts to cry.

"Why didn't you tell me this before?" he says.

"It was too hard. It took me a while to figure out what was wrong, and then it was too hard to tell you. You've been through all this shit that hasn't been your fault. I didn't want to add one more thing."

"So you just removed yourself from me, went away so I couldn't reach you? That added the biggest thing. All this physical stuff is nothing contrasted to your not being there for me."

"I'm sorry. It took me so long to figure out and then I didn't know how to say it."

"You just did. And it's not like there isn't anything we can do about it. Dr. Silkiss says my right eye will become dominant if I go without the patch; it will take over for my left and the double vision may become almost imperceptible. I can call her to find out more. I'll go without the patch if that will help us. I just want you close to me."

"I want the same thing. I feel shallow; I don't want to be the kind of person who allows a physical thing to affect how I feel, but that damned eye patch means that I can't see you and in some ways you can't see me. I want a glass of wine. I feel as if my insides are a jumble."

I get up and open the cupboard to grab a bottle of Syrah and a glass. As I go to the drawer for an opener, Arthur gets up, comes over and wraps his arms around me.

"I just need you to hold me — emotionally as well as physically," he says. "That's the only important thing."

He takes off his eye patch and puts it on the counter.

"I will figure out how to see without this. I can't have it be a wall between us."

Arthur is as good as his word. He is going without his patch, although he tells me he will continue to wear it, at least for a while, when he is at work and otherwise not with me.

Wally woke us up this morning to tell us his dream in which he made friends with a wolf. Wally says the wolf rubbed his head against his leg and then let Wally pet him. Wally and the wolf went into the forest together; however, a hunter came along and shot the wolf, but the wolf's spirit came back and helped Wally, helped him do things. Wally and the spirit ended up living together in a house with the dead wolf's body.

Arthur and I are sitting on the sofa in the family room on a Sunday night, decompressing from the weekend. We all went to Monterey, our first trip since Arthur's most recent leg surgery. He is fine but tired. We are all tired; Wally is already in bed.

"Quiet," I say. "Do you hear that?"

I turn down the TV and listen to a scraping, raspy sound, like feet scrabbling over wood surfaces.

"That's the icemaker," says Arthur.

"Are you sure? That sounds more like something moving in the wall behind the refrigerator," I say, turning to look at him.

"Would you stop?" he says. "I'm sure; it's just the icemaker."

I am willing to go with this explanation because I want the noise to be the icemaker, not what I imagine might be exploring the territory within our walls.

I believe the night noises are creaks in the floorboards, a faulty vent, the house rattling its bones, until early Thursday morning while grinding beans for coffee, I notice bite marks on peaches and tomatoes left on the counter overnight. I look around and see bread torn apart and then find pellets on the floor next to the dog food. Maybe they're mice, I say to myself—little things with twitchy noses, creatures portrayed on cutesy sweaters and hats with pom-poms. But these pellets are big.

"Oh, the rats are terrible in the hills this year, must be all the rain we've had. Everybody's got them."

This is what the exterminator tells me over the phone. He specializes in rodents and is booked until Monday because of the burgeoning rat population.

"What am I supposed to do until then?" I ask.

"Put away all food all the time, everything — dog food, people food, fish food."

"What about traps? Can I put down traps?"

"If you want to," he says, "but don't get too excited about it. I'll take care of everything when I get there."

I have *rats* in my house. How am I supposed to not get excited? I have to do something. I go to an Ace Hardware store and buy Rat Zappers — battery-operated electrocuting traps, some steel wool, giant wooden traps, rolls of duct tape, a different gauge of steel wool, plug-in noise emanators that will repel rodents, packages of rat poison, and a huge galvanized-steel garbage can to put it all in.

I drive home and start working. I want to get this finished before Wally gets home from school, figuring that because he's ten, he will either be freaked out by the notion of rats or he will want to make them into pets. Or he will spin this rat thing into some kind of futuristic fantasy in which rat creatures, Ratataurs, maybe, confound logic and cause mayhem in the galaxy.

I clean everything — with bleach, with cleanser, with Murphy's Oil Soap. I blast Calexico on the stereo, but I hear rat paws clicking over the surface of my home. I imagine rats coming out and skittering over the floors the way they skittered over the surface of the ship transporting Count Dracula from the Carpathian Mountains to England, the way they streamed onto the streets of Whitby when the boat ran aground. I work with a scrub brush and rags and paper towels — now I'm wearing headphones so the band's sound can make quicker contact with my brain. I try to focus on the surfaces, but the rats have extended beyond the exterior: they are taking up mental residence. I want to know where they go during the day. I want to know where they were before they came to my house. I want to know their favorite food. I want to know where they nest.

Not in my house. My house has had all of its bones broken and it is only now healing. My house is Arthur's body after our car was hit — multiple breaks in every limb, broken ribs, his eye bulging out from a fistula. My house is recovering from a head injury that doesn't resolve itself for six weeks. Rats cannot live in my house.

I have to stop. I have to break away from this. Wally needs to be picked up from school, and soon after that Arthur will be home to pack for his trip to D.C. tomorrow. Arthur flying across the country is a miracle to me, when three years ago he couldn't walk across the room, couldn't have a conversation, couldn't hold a pencil let alone know what to do with it. Now he spends so much time zipping around to work that some days it feels as if I have lost him anyway.

In the years since the accident, Arthur and I have been so preoccupied with surviving, with helping each other stay alive, that we have traveled parallel paths. We deal with our medical needs, attend to Wally, and work. While we do these things in concert, we do not do them together in the way we always thought of ourselves as together. I remember the psychologist who told us, shortly after Arthur recovered his cognitive functions, that most marriages in which both parties have had head injuries have a ninety-eight percent rate of failing. Who the hell measures these things? How many marriages are there where both parties have had head injuries?

I e-mail my friend George, who teaches business ethics to grad students, thinking he could have some insight about the rats, about my anxiety. George knows how to make me feel better. He's been good at that in recent years, although when we were lovers years ago in Moscow, he knew how to torture me so I could barely breathe. He writes back: "Rats are one way to go. I would have chosen roaches myself, but rats are bigger and juicier. Because roaches are smaller, however, you can have so many more of them. Knowing anything is in the interpretation; I am not sure how to interpret rats. I know what roaches mean to me; I could guess what rats mean to you, but that would be me projecting my roaches onto your rats—a precarious psychological game at best and almost certain to result in false meanings."

I leave to pick up Wally at school, hoping he won't sense my anxiety. I tell him I've bought the traps and zappers for mice, afraid to say rats. He looks me straight in the eye when I say that.

"Why are you trying to kill them?" he asks. "You

won't even kill spiders. Why would you kill animals?"

By the time we get home, Arthur is already there. He has brought dinner — Thai spring rolls, satay, rice noodles, a green curry. I grab him for a minute before we sit down and give him the low-down on the rats, tell him about the exterminator. I speak quietly, so Wally won't hear.

"Listen," says Arthur, "I'm only going away for three days. I'll help you with this when I get back."

Arthur has always wanted to be the good guy in my life, the guy who doesn't torture, who doesn't fail me. But he is leaving.

Before we go to bed I set traps and zappers in the kitchen, dining room, and living room and near the hot water heater in the basement. I lie awake listening for the invasion. They are scurrying up the walls, fighting for entrance into the house, scratching at each other's faces. In the morning, Arthur checks the traps. I dally in the bedroom, figuring the longer he's gone, the better chance there is we've caught something. He comes back smiling.

"We have success," he says. "Apparently the zappers work. There was a rat in the one in the kitchen, so you can relax while I'm away."

"That can't be the only one."

"Maybe not," he says, "but at least they should get the message that this isn't a safe place for them. Look, I can help you with this next week, but I can't cancel this trip right now."

After Arthur leaves and I take Wally to school, I go online to find links between rats and psychology — there are hundreds. This must be a popular topic: psychologists are looking for a variety of papers on rats. I find Freud's "Rat Man"; I learn about torture using rats to eat body parts. I remember an episode of a TV show, *La Femme Nikita*, in which this happens — beautiful, blonde Peta Wilson with her head in a rat crate. I remember George Orwell's *1984* and my frightened thrill the first time I watched Fritz Murnau's 1922 film *Nosferatu*. The vampire had rat teeth — two incisors on the top. I can't remember if he had bottom incisors, but in rats those are even longer and stronger than the top ones. And they grow — not in the movie, in real life — rat teeth never stop growing, so rats have to keep gnawing on things to keep their teeth from spiraling out into the world.

At the library, I read essays about rats and children of abusive parents. And now I'm onto cannibalism. If I've got this right, children whose parents are consistently unable to meet their emotional needs see themselves as wanting too much. When their needs are never fulfilled, the children start to believe that meeting their desires would essentially devour their parents. Since these children can't stand the idea of eating their parents alive, they teach themselves not to have wants in order to survive. I imagine little rat children whose teeth keep growing and eventually wind around their heads until growing back into their skulls.

Psychologist John B. Watson conducted research in 1920 in which a nine-month-old boy named Albert was subjected to experiments involving a white rat and fear response. This was the beginning of behaviorism. We're afraid of rats because they are too close to us. We can feel their aggression, their insatiable appetites, their need to take over a place.

I sort out the weekend into rat stages and Wally stages. In the Wally stages, my son has a stomach virus and starts throwing up Saturday morning. We watch *The Lord of the Rings* trilogy together, him sleeping off and on during the days, eating small amounts of chicken soup and crackers. In the rat stages, I find more carcasses.

The way the zappers work is that a red bulb on top of the box lights up when the zapper is turned on. If an animal is caught and electrocuted, the light starts to blink, so you know right away there's something in the box. In theory, all you have to do is pick up the trap, take it to the trash can, and dump the contents into the garbage. Lights are blinking both Saturday and Sunday mornings — in the kitchen and the basement. When I see the first blinking light, my insides freeze. I put on a pair of rubber gloves, walk over to the trap, listen for movement and, hearing none, pick up the metal box. I carry the trap out to the trash can, but before I turn it over, I have to look inside. There is a small rat, its head at the far end of the trap, so I see mostly tail and tail end. This reminds me of a Halloween toy — the black skull with a rat's tail coming out of one eye socket and its red-eyed head coming out the other. I dump the carcass. There are two more like this. Two blinking traps turn out to be empty, their potential victims escapees. When Arthur gets home Sunday evening, I tell him I am a collector, one who buries plague rats from the Middle Ages.

Monday morning, I am relieved to find no new rodentia. After getting Wally situated in his room for the day, home because he still has a stomach virus, I welcome the first exterminator. Arthur is working at home, and has called a second exterminator to come later in the morning.

The first rat expert is about fifty-five years old, solid, speaks with authority.

"You have to set traps in the basement and all around the property," he says. "I have traps all around my perimeter, so I get them before they get to the house. And I never see rats."

He walks around the house with me, tells me that I'll have to "get those bay laurel branches cut back. Can't have branches going to the roof—they can get to the house that way. And you're going to have to replace that garage door. See the space between the door and the ground? A rat can get in there; doesn't look like much, but they can squeeze themselves into almost nothing, flatten right out. I've seen them get through spaces I wouldn't have believed. I'll set out poison traps today, and then I'll come back next week and see where the activity is."

He gets half a dozen ten-inch-square black plastic boxes with hinged closures and holes on the sides. He shows me that the boxes close tightly to keep other animals from opening them. I want to know what happens if a rat eats the poison and then dies in the wall or something.

"If that happens, you'll smell it. They smell pretty bad

when they're dead. You smell it, you call me," he tells me. "I'll come out and get it. That's part of the service."

The next rat specialist will show at one o'clock, but I have another appointment, so Arthur handles that one. When I return home, about four o'clock, I find Arthur sitting at the kitchen table with Bryan, the contractor who has done work on our house since we've lived here. Bryan has replaced doors, windows, toilets, floors. He's a steady guy who gets things done.

"Why don't you sit down and listen to this too," says Arthur. "I was just about to describe to Bryan what the rat guy told me we had to do to get rid of them."

"Wait a minute. He told you we could get rid of them?"

"Yes, but it takes more than setting traps. He says if we want to keep the rats out, we need to run eighteen inches of wire mesh around the base of the house, from the foundation down, so they can't dig through to get into the basement."

"How are we supposed to do that?" I ask.

"That's what Bryan is going to tell us," says Arthur.

Bryan has a voice like Zeus — deep and commanding — so I believe him when he says it will be a pain, but he can have some of his crew come over later this week and dig down and attach the mesh around the foundation.

"A couple of days," says Bryan, when I ask how long it will take, "but it's going to cost a lot more than traps. Probably around three thousand dollars."

"Shit," I say. "We can't afford that."

"But you think it will work?" says Arthur to Bryan.

"I can't swear to it, but it makes more sense than any-thing else I've heard about how to keep rats out."

"Okay," says Arthur, "then do it. As soon as possible."

As Arthur sees Bryan out, I make a cup of tea and am sitting at the table again when he comes back in. He sits down.

"How are we going to pay for this?" I say to him.

Arthur gives me a look I haven't seen in three years, like he's going to be in charge of this, like he wants to be the guy dealing with the problem.

"This is making you crazy, and as far as I'm con-cerned, this is what money is for. If we can spend three thousand dollars — even if we have to borrow it — and it will make that panic and anxiety on your face go away, we're going to do it. You can't live like this, so Wally and I can't live like this either. We need to get rid of the rats."

The part of me that pays bills says no, we can't do this, but that part is quickly overridden by a sense of relief the size of the planet Zorgon. I give myself up to this moment of being taken care of, an old need met. I don't want to feel like I'm cannibalizing someone just because I want something. I look at Arthur and see who he is now — not a crumpled heap who has been pasted back together by surgeons and psychologists. I see a person I love telling me that I don't have to be the only one standing guard at the gates.

## EVERYTHING THAT RISES OR *EINIGE KREISE*\*

*\*Some Circles*, the title of a 1926 painting
by Wassily Kandinsky

Dervs refuses to tell this story. She thinks it is a little nuts. This took place in the East Bay hills, where Dervs walked with Vinnie every day that she could, not so much walked as hiked, three to six miles a day depending on how much time she could free. One of those days, she and Vinnie, whose broken leg had neatly mended, hiked about two miles in to a meadow, a hill really, covered with grass and small flowers, and began to walk to the top. After a few steps, Dervs stopped and, for no reason she could think of, raised her right arm almost straight up, but not so far that she couldn't see it. She looked at the end of her hand, the end of her forefinger actually, and was amazed to see a balloon coming out of her finger, a balloon shaped like a little girl with brown hair and wearing a brown-and-black plaid dress. The balloon girl's right forefinger was touching Dervs's finger as the girl floated upside down. The girl was getting bigger, becoming more of a balloon while Dervs watched. As the balloon girl grew, Dervs wondered who this was, this apparition balloon, and as she wondered, the balloon girl detached from the tip of Dervs's finger and began to float away, upwards. Dervs watched her, she who started small and grew large, grow small again as she floated toward the sun, as she became a spot in

311

front of the sun and floated out of sight.

Dervs couldn't figure it out, but I can tell you that this balloon was both Dervs's mother and Dervs herself as a child devoid of a future. This particular Dervs child, the one without the future, was leaving, and these two, the mother and the child, became circles as they moved away, circles expanding and contracting, taking on colors both warm and cool, as they journeyed into space, separate and together, leaving Dervs and her dog standing among the flowers and insects on the meadow soil.

Arthur and I have taken seats in an old assembly room of the Student Union. The building was designed by California architect Julia Morgan, and it smells of the dark wood that covers walls, floor, ceiling. The morning sun comes through the windows, turning everything into slow-moving caramel. We look through the commencement program — from the group photo of the fifth-grade graduates on the cover to the schedule — ending with the statements each of the fifth graders has written as a conclusion to his or her time at Mills. As we read Wally's statement, both Arthur and I are looking for signs of psychological damage as a result of the accident, but Wally writes about a camping trip and the class sleepover in the fourth-grade classroom:

> Everybody in my class and I went to a field and played flashlight tag, which was a blast! Then we went to Lake Aliso, which is my favorite spot on campus. It is so beautiful. (He thanks his teachers and friends and us.) I would like to thank my dad for all the hard work he did with helping me prepare for the ICEE test. I would also like to thank my mom for helping me through everything from homework to problems with my friends.

This is where the day resides for me, in this last sentence. This is where these last years reside for me. This sentence tells me I am a valuable parent. I will not have my mother's death and I do not have my mother's life. My child's life is nothing like my childhood. My son has a strong sense of who he is. He is not afraid of what he wants, needs, desires, cherishes. He knows that he is loved and that his life was not destroyed by a traffic crash.

Arthur and I are like all the other parents, waiting to see how wonderful our child looks walking through the graduates' doorway, reading his speech, accepting his certificate of completion. And we joke with each other about how funny it is to have a fifth-grade graduation.

Arthur says, "What, we didn't expect him to finish fifth grade?"

We are like all the other parents. We are laughing and taking photographs and happy to see Wally goofing around with his friends. We hold hands; we are alive in the moment.

We are like all the other parents out on the lawn after the ceremony, lining up for the potluck food, sitting on the grass balancing paper plates and talking about what our children looked like in preschool, which of their quirks have survived since then, talking to people we may never see again because our children will be going on to different schools.

Nearly four years have passed since the accident, and that whole time all we wanted was to be like other families. We wanted to have time to think about trivialities, to sit in the sun and eat lunch, to pick an ant off a paper plate.

We do not want to look like Frankenstein's monster or the bald lady or a pirate. Today, I believe we are a rubber orchestra — having bounced back from disaster, the lip of destruction and obliteration. Wally is going into sixth grade next year, and we are all looking forward, beyond this minute. We are behaving as if we have a future.

*July 2006*

CPSIA information can be obtained at www.ICGtesting.com
Printed in the USA
LVOW10*2149100615

442034LV00009B/46/P